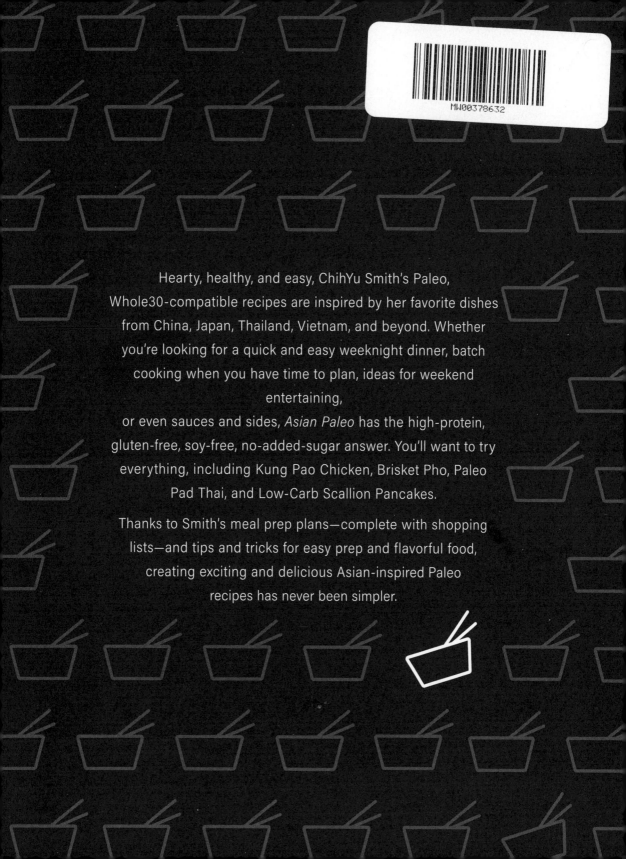

Hearty, healthy, and easy, ChihYu Smith's Paleo, Whole30-compatible recipes are inspired by her favorite dishes from China, Japan, Thailand, Vietnam, and beyond. Whether you're looking for a quick and easy weeknight dinner, batch cooking when you have time to plan, ideas for weekend entertaining,
or even sauces and sides, *Asian Paleo* has the high-protein, gluten-free, soy-free, no-added-sugar answer. You'll want to try everything, including Kung Pao Chicken, Brisket Pho, Paleo Pad Thai, and Low-Carb Scallion Pancakes.

Thanks to Smith's meal prep plans—complete with shopping lists—and tips and tricks for easy prep and flavorful food, creating exciting and delicious Asian-inspired Paleo recipes has never been simpler.

MW00378632

ASIAN PALEO

ASIAN PALEO

EASY, FRESH RECIPES TO MAKE AHEAD OR ENJOY RIGHT NOW FROM I HEART♥ UMAMI

CHIHYU SMITH

The Countryman Press
A division of W. W. Norton & Company
Independent Publishers Since 1923

Chicken Yakisoba, page 133

CONTENTS

INTRODUCTION 9
THE ASIAN-INSPIRED PALEO PANTRY 15

Low-Carb Scallion Pancakes,
page 175

INTRODUCTION

I GREW UP IN KAOHSIUNG, TAIWAN, A SEAPORT TOWN IN THE SOUTHERN PART OF THE ISLAND. Both sides of my family immigrated to Taiwan from China after World War II. To a Chinese family, food means everything and is the center of our daily life. As in so many modern families, both my parents were working professionals; still, even without much time to cook, my mom managed to prepare fresh and nutritious homemade meals for my brother and me every single day. So, quick yet healthy meals were a huge part of my early life.

Years later, I moved to New York City for graduate school and met my husband, Nate. I landed a very demanding job and was attending grad school at night, and although I cooked occasionally on the weekend, most nights we would order takeout. Getting home for dinner around ten p.m. and eating greasy delivery food with tons of carbs and thick sauces that were either too salty or too sweet, I noticed that not only was I starting to gain weight, but I also felt bloated, sluggish, and tired all the time.

After a couple of years, I was sick of feeling this way, so I started setting a little time aside to make homemade meals a higher priority for my husband and me. I started bringing healthier food to work and making smarter choices when I ordered takeout.

I stumbled upon the Paleo world completely by accident. I was searching for health food trends and discovered the word "Paleo." At the time I didn't know what it meant and thought it was just another trend that would soon burn out. Yes, I was skeptical at first.

All I wanted was to look younger and feel fitter while feeding my family delicious, honest, good food without spending too much time in the kitchen. But soon I realized that Paleo was not just another fad diet that would leave me hungry or a quick weight-loss solution without long-term results. Paleo has taught me how to balance my diet and what food makes me feel my best, gives me the most energy, and is less likely to cause sugar cravings or sudden blood sugar spikes and crashes. Thinking about food in this way has also taught me to be a responsible consumer when it comes to food: to get to know local farmers and small business owners and support ethical, sustainable farming.

When I adopted the Paleo lifestyle, I wanted to make food that was best optimized for our health, using nutrient-dense, minimally processed ingredients, high-quality protein, and fiber to keep us nourished, and low-carbohydrate foods and no added sugar to help regulate our blood sugar level. I also wanted to replicate what I grew up eating with my mom and my grandmother in Taiwan, but without relying on store-bought bottles filled with unnatural and unnecessary ingredients. I wanted to make food that wasn't filled with sugar and gloopy, shiny starch that, collectively, sends our health on a downward spiral.

With Paleo, I lost unwanted body fat and no longer felt sluggish after lunch. These changes inspired me to start my own blog—and now to write my first cookbook—so I can help other people feel the same way. Most important, I want to share how delicious, fun, and exciting meals in an Asian-inspired Paleo kitchen can be.

On my blog, *I Heart Umami*, I share Asian-inspired Paleo, Whole30, and Keto recipes. My taste buds are naturally drawn to savory flavors (*umami* means "savory deliciousness" in Japanese), and *I Heart Umami* became my channel to share my own, Paleo-friendly take on the foods I grew up eating. I also started a meal-planning program called Cook

Once Eat All Week, where I help families to plan healthy, nutritious, and delicious Paleo meals that fit into their lives realistically.

We all have our own definitions of what *healthy* means. So, I'm not here to preach. But if you're reading this book, chances are you're curious, or maybe longing for a happier, healthier you, and wrestling with a subject matter that can be emotional for all of us: food. Homemade meals made from scratch are a form of love. They remind us of family and culture, and show us where we came from. Meals don't need to be complicated or "sophisticated," or use obscure ingredients. Think of cooking as a fun opportunity to experiment, create, follow your imagination, and find your own definition of *healthy*. I hope this book will open the door to a wide variety of Asian-inspired flavors and awaken your taste buds in your everyday cooking.

I created these dishes based on my memories of growing up in Taiwan, where the cuisine is so diverse, with influences from neighboring countries, including China, Japan, Korea, Thailand, Vietnam, Malaysia, Singapore, and the Philippines. These recipes reflect who I am and where I came from, but since I have been living in the States for almost twenty years, you'll find that the ingredients I use are easy to find (see page 15 for the staples of my Asian-inspired Paleo pantry).

All the recipes are free of gluten, wheat, rice, grains, dairy, soy, and added sugar. I use coconut aminos to replace soy sauce or tamari; fish sauce and shiitake mushrooms to add extra savory umami taste; apples and other fruit to add natural sweetness. You'll find my love for using aromatics (garlic, ginger, shallots, scallions) to make my dishes so flavorful and so fragrant sets these dishes apart from others. I even went one step further to make the recipes in this cookbook Whole30-friendly, by excluding what even Paleo practitioners consider healthy sweeteners—honey, coconut sugar, and maple syrup—because if there's a way to achieve an equally delicious (if not even better) flavor without added sweeteners, why not share that option?

THIS BOOK HAS FIVE SECTIONS:

1 WEEKNIGHT BFF

These are dishes that take no time (and little prep time) to make. They are my family's go-to weeknight dinners, nutrient-dense and full of flavor. They include Protein-Packed Fluffy Egg Drop Soup, Paleo Chicken Katsu, Healthy Teriyaki Chicken, Beef and Broccoli, Thai-Inspired Paleo Salmon Cakes, and more.

2 BATCH COOKING PERFECT

This chapter includes recipes that are perfect for batch-cooking in advance, such as Vietnamese Brisket Pho, Sweet-and-Sour Chicken, and Chinese Pepper Steak. My notes and tips for making ahead will save you tons of time during the work week.

3 WEEKEND FUN

These dishes are perfect for entertaining. From Chicken Yakisoba (Japanese-inspired stir-fry "noodles") to Filipino Skirt Steak and Cauliflower Fried Rice, these dishes are perfect for brunch and movie nights, and are fun for the entire family to make.

4 EASY ADD-ONS

These add-ons range from vegetables and side dishes, such as Shiitake Mushroom and Baby Bok Choy Stir-Fry, to good carbohydrates, such as Smoky Curly Sweet Potato Noodle Fries. They are great plug-in dishes that will go well with any of the main dishes in this book.

5 **FLAVOR POP**

I Heart Umami sauces is a collection of my favorite healthy homemade sauces that will take a dish from ordinary to fabulous! You'll find my signature sauces: Sesame Chicken Sauce, Umami Dim Sum Dumpling Dipping Sauce, Teriyaki Sauce, and more.

For me, it wasn't enough to create a beautiful book. But a book you can actually use, and which will help you reduce your intake of sugar, fried foods, and empty carbs while optimizing your health and satisfying your cravings, *was* worth writing. So, whether you grew up in Asia like me, are an enthusiast for Asian food, or are seeking better and healthier meals for your family, get ready for a wide variety of truly flavorful and mouthwatering simple homemade meals coming from your very own Asian-inspired Paleo kitchen.

HAVE FUN, SIT BACK, AND ENJOY YOUR LOVELY MEALS. IT'S THAT EASY!

THE ASIAN-INSPIRED PALEO PANTRY

ASIAN-INSPIRED PALEO COOKING IS QUITE SIMPLE. For the recipes in this book and on my blog, almost all the ingredients can be purchased at your local grocery store, and a few specialty items are easy to find online. (These pantry items are also Whole30-friendly!) I always put myself in the shoes of my readers who might not have quick access to certain ingredients, such as fresh lemongrass, Thai holy basil, galangal, Thai chiles . . . and so on. My goal is to remove as many hurdles as possible so that you can enjoy simple and delicious homemade food and feel good about what you are feeding yourself and your family.

The following pantry guide includes the staple items that I use on a daily basis. You can find most of these ingredients at Whole Foods Market, and all of them are available from online retailers.

GO-TO SEASONINGS, SAUCES, AND COOKING OILS

COCONUT SECRET COCONUT AMINOS: Coconut aminos are a great substitute for soy sauce. They're made from sap that comes from the coconut blossom. They are gluten- and soy-free, with a lighter taste than soy sauce or tamari. I like to use them for marinades and add them to stir-fry dishes, soup, or practically anywhere I'd like to boost a little umami. Throughout this book, you'll see how and where I use coconut aminos to extract natural sweetness from cooking. This little bottle is one of my secrets in making Asian-inspired Paleo cuisine without using added sugar.

RED BOAT FISH SAUCE: Fish sauce, made from salted and fermented anchovies, is a staple in Thai, Vietnamese, and Malaysian cuisine. It is used almost like salt. If you use fish sauce, I'd recommend you reduce the amount of added salt as fish sauce can be quite salty. Use it sparingly; a few drops will go a long way. A good bottle of fish sauce—such as Red Boat brand—is a light to medium amber color and has a longer fermentation process so it tastes less fishy. Many brands have a very strong and unpleasant smell and contain processed ingredients. I recommend using only Red Boat for cooking. Fish sauce is great for Vietnamese dipping sauce, noodles, or stir-fry and curry dishes. I also like to use it as a beef marinade. Store it in the refrigerator once opened.

LA TOURANGELLE TOASTED SESAME OIL: Growing up in Asia, I had never seen untoasted sesame oil, so when I first saw it in the States I was intrigued. That said, whenever I refer to sesame oil in my recipes, I always mean toasted sesame oil, because that's how people use it—in toasted form—back home. Look for clarity in the oil bottle: the oil should not be cloudy. One with a dark amber color will have a stronger fragrance than the lighter version. Use sparingly; a little goes a long way. Use for seasoning, in salad dressing, or to marinate meats.

CHOSEN FOODS AVOCADO OIL: I fell in love with avocado oil because of its high smoke point and neutral flavor. It's great for stir-frying and is vegetarian- and vegan-friendly. I use it to replace soy, canola, sunflower, or any vegetable oils.

MARUKAN RICE VINEGAR: There are a few types of rice vinegar. Look for white rice vinegar with a clear to light yellowish color. It is made from fermented rice and has a milder (less acidity) and naturally sweeter taste than other vinegars. Check that it has no added sulfites or other additives. Rice vinegar is common in Asian cuisine. I like to use it sparingly in salads, dressing, and dipping sauce for dumplings.

WHOLE FOODS MARKET BALSAMIC AND AGED BALSAMIC VINEGARS: By complete coincidence, I discovered that balsamic and aged balsamic are great substitutes for Chinese black vinegar, which is made from wheat, millet, and sorghum, ingredients that aren't Paleo or Whole30 compliant. Black vinegar also often has too many processed additives.

Although balsamic and aged balsamic vinegar do not taste the same as black vinegar, they're a much healthier choice and, when used correctly (combined with other seasonings and aromatics), they taste just as good as the traditional black vinegar.

ENTUBE HARISSA CHILI PASTE: I discovered Entube harissa paste while I was looking for a substitute for Sichuan black bean sauce. It does not taste the same as real black bean sauce, but again, when you use it in the right context along with aromatics and the right cooking methods, this harissa paste is an awesome substitute for anyone who follows a Paleo or Whole30 diet. You'll see that I use it in many Sichuan-inspired recipes in this cookbook.

THAI KITCHEN RED CURRY PASTE: I use Thai Kitchen red curry paste supplemented by my homemade Curry Flavor Enhancer (page 184). Why? I rarely make curry just by using store-bought curry paste. It's not as fragrant, fresh, or lively. What's the solution? I blend my own mixture, using fresh shallots, garlic, cilantro or parsley, chiles, ginger (or galangal, if you can find it) . . . and so on. When you see how easy and fragrant it is to make my Curry Flavor Enhancer, you'll never make a pot of homemade curry without my recipe!

OTHER STAPLES IN MY PANTRY

A&B AMERICAN-STYLE HOT SAUCE, ORIGINAL FLAVOR: This is a great, all-natural hot sauce made with fresh red Fresno chile peppers without added sugar or artificial preservatives. I use it in my recipes, from sweet-and-spicy chili dipping sauce for Malaysian crispy chicken wings to stir-fry dishes.

ALMOND BUTTER, CASHEW BUTTER, SUNFLOWER SEED BUTTER: Most often I use nut or seed butter in conjunction with tahini to create a more complex flavor of Chinese-inspired sesame sauce. Check the label and ingredients for a nut or seed butter that has a no-added-sugar version. Sunflower seed butter (like SunButter) is a great nut-free choice if you are allergic to nuts.

APPLESAUCE (UNSWEETENED): I don't use it often but applesauce is a great natural sweetener for sauce, beef marinade, and so on.

BOB'S RED MILL ARROWROOT STARCH: Arrowroot starch, extracted from the roots of the arrowroot plant, is an easily digested grain- and gluten-free ingredient perfect for gluten-free baking. I use it as a thickener for sauces, soups, and stews, or to replace cornstarch for dusting meat.

COCONUT MILK (FULL-FAT, CANNED): I tasted several brands of coconut milk and by far WholeFoods 365 tastes the best to me. Stir (or blend) it well before using.

GHEE: Ghee is a form of highly clarified butter that contains fewer dairy proteins than regular butter. It is traditionally used in Indian and South Asian cooking. Because ghee does not contain the same levels of dairy protein as butter, it's better for people who do not tolerate dairy products well. My favorite brand is Fourth and Heart Ghee Butter Original Recipe.

TAHINI: Tahini is pure sesame paste. It should not contain any added sugar, so check its ingredients list. I love using it to re-create Asian-inspired creamy "noodle" sauce and in salad dressing. So delicious!

SPICES/DRIED HERBS/ETC.

TAE-KYUNG KOREAN RED PEPPER POWDER (GOCHUGARU): *Gochugaru* is
milder than cayenne pepper, with a hint of sweetness. If you use a lot in one dish, it can be spicy. Usually I use these flakes sparingly. Most often I sprinkle them on chicken breasts or steak for grilling. It gives the meat a lovely color.

WHOLE STAR ANISE: Star anise is used to flavor curries and beef stews.
Its name originated from its starlike shape. It tastes similar to fennel, but is much stronger, so use sparingly. I often add it to stock and stews—use only a few pieces (one to two) and discard before serving.

BURMA SPICE SICHUAN (FLOWER) PEPPERCORNS: Sichuan flower
peppercorns have a lemony flavor and a gently, pleasantly numbing mouthfeel. The closest way I can describe their flavor is, it's as if lemon and black pepper had a baby together. They're used in Sichuan-style cuisine and sometimes I grind the peppercorns (using a coffee grinder) to add to meatballs. Select red peppercorns that are bright in color. Use sparingly; a little goes a long way. They're commonly used for lamb stir-fry dishes.

DRIED SHIITAKE MUSHROOMS: Dried shiitake mushrooms can keep for a long time in a sealed container in the refrigerator, or in a cool, dark, dry area. Select whole mushrooms, not presliced ones. Also, select thick mushrooms with white fissures—the more fissures, the better.

Dried shiitake mushrooms require soaking before cooking. Soak the mushrooms in room-temperature water in the morning and you'll be able to slice and use them by the afternoon. You can also soak them in hot water to cut the time in half. The shiitake soaking water contains tons of umami flavor, too! Just filter the water with a sieve before using it. You can freeze the soaking water in ice cube trays to pop out and store in freezer bags for soup stock and broth.

GOJI BERRIES: I love goji berries! They are adorable and delicious. How do I use them? I learned from my mother, who adds them to Chinese chicken soup or bone broth. They add a little natural sweetness and are a wonderful addition to the kitchen.

JUJUBE DATES (CHINESE/KOREAN RED DATES, DRIED): These can be used as a sweetener, much like goji berries. These are much larger dates, in dried form. We add them to chicken, beef, or pork bone stew or broth to add natural sweetness and fragrance. Discard them before serving. There's no need to rehydrate them before adding them to the soup pot.

ROOT AND SPRING CHINESE HERBAL SOUP PACKS: When I was growing up in Asia, my mom would not make Chinese chicken herbal soup, bone broth, pork bone soup, and so on, without adding Chinese dried herbal packs. Now, there are many varieties when it comes to Chinese dried herbs and it's difficult to find good-quality herbs. Since I moved to the States, I was very happy when I discovered Root and Spring, a Los Angeles–based Hong Kongese herbal store that ships really high-quality Chinese dried herbs worldwide. I used its Chinese Herbal Soup Mix

for Good Health and Immunity in my Electric Pressure Cooker Chinese Chicken Bone Broth (page 64). It's a must-have in every Asian household. The Chinese Herbal Soup Mix from Root and Spring includes astragalus root (*huang qi*), codonopsis root (*dang shen*), dried Chinese yam (*huai shan*), dried goji berries (*gou qi zi*), longan (*longyan*), and red dates (*hong zao*). The goji berries, Chinese yam, and longan are all edible.

BATCH COOK

WEEKEND

EASY

FLAVOR

NIGHT BFF

ING PERFECT

FUN

ADD-ONS

POP

Dan Dan Sesame Noodles,
page 50

Weeknight Best Friend Forever! Who doesn't love easy, fresh meals that are quick to put together? These recipes are my back-pocket dishes when I don't have time to plan in advance. Although these meals may be simple and quick to make, they are loaded with flavor and nutrition. Pack leftovers for the next day's lunch to power you through the day!

VIETNAMESE PHO-INSPIRED TOMATO BEEF SOUP

ACTIVE TIME: 30 MINUTES | SERVES 4

BEEF:

¾ to 1 pound beef sirloin

2 teaspoons crushed garlic

¼ teaspoon freshly ground black pepper

2 teaspoons fish sauce (Red Boat brand preferred)

2 teaspoons extra virgin olive oil

SOUP:

1 tablespoon coconut or avocado oil

3 large garlic cloves, finely chopped

3 teaspoons finely chopped fresh ginger

3 scallions, chopped and separated into white parts and green parts

Salt

6 cups beef stock

2 teaspoons fish sauce (Red Boat brand preferred)

2 teaspoons rice vinegar

1½ teaspoons coconut aminos

2 tomatoes, sliced into wedges, a few pieces reserved for garnish

Zest of ½ lime

Zest of ½ lemon

TO SERVE:

Juice of ¼ to ½ lime

Fresh cilantro (optional)

This recipe is inspired by traditional Vietnamese pho. The tomato adds a lovely citrusy flavor along with lime juice, lime zest, and ginger to mimic lemongrass. Just like your favorite pho from the restaurant, but made simpler!

1. MARINATE THE BEEF: Freeze the beef for 20 to 30 minutes, then slice paper thin and place in a bowl. Add the remaining beef ingredients and marinate for 10 to 15 minutes (or overnight in the refrigerator).

2. PREPARE THE SOUP: Heat the coconut oil in a wok or medium soup pot over medium-high heat, then lower the heat to medium. Stir-fry the garlic, ginger, and white scallion parts. Season with a small pinch of salt. Sauté until fragrant, about 90 seconds. Add the beef stock, fish sauce, rice vinegar, coconut aminos, and tomato. Cover, bring to a boil, then lower the heat and simmer for about 5 minutes.

3. Just before serving, bring the soup back to a boil. Add the marinated beef and simmer for about 30 seconds, or just until the beef turns light pink (see note). Turn off the heat. Add the lime and lemon zest.

4. TASTE AND ADJUST THE SEASONINGS: Season with lime juice to taste and add more coconut aminos or coarse salt, if desired. Garnish with the reserved tomato, cilantro, if using, and green scallion parts. Serve hot.

Note

Add the beef to the simmering soup right before you are about to serve this dish. Simmering the thin slices for 30 seconds will leave them half cooked, just as in restaurant pho.

PROTEIN-PACKED FLUFFY EGG DROP SOUP

ACTIVE TIME: 20 TO 25 MINUTES | SERVES 3

1 teaspoon ghee

1 teaspoon minced fresh ginger

2 scallions, chopped and separated into white and green parts

⅓ to ½ pound ground chicken, turkey, or pork

1 cup sliced fresh shiitake mushrooms (or more if you'd like)

Salt

3 cups chicken stock

1 tablespoon coconut aminos

¼ teaspoon ground cumin

3 large eggs

Cherry tomatoes, halved (optional)

Toasted sesame oil

Egg drop soup is such a common dish in many Asian households and each region has a slightly different take on it. I added ground meat for more protein to keep you full longer. The meat also adds extra umami deliciousness. This is a quick and healthy soup that makes a perfect starter or light supper.

1. In a medium, heavy-bottomed soup pot over medium-high heat, add the ghee, ginger, and white scallion parts and sauté until fragrant.

2. Add the ground chicken and mushrooms and sauté until the meat is cooked through and the mushrooms turn soft, about 5 minutes. Season with salt to taste.

3. Add the chicken stock, coconut aminos, and cumin. Increase the heat and bring to a boil.

4. Meanwhile, prepare the fluffy egg drops: Gently whisk the eggs for about 30 seconds in a bowl (try not to overwhisk). Hold chopsticks or a fork against one side of the bowl. From that side, slowly drizzle the eggs into the boiling soup in a swirling motion. Let the eggs stand for a few seconds to take shape in the boiling soup, and then gently whisk the broth and eggs to finish cooking.

5. Add the cherry tomatoes, if using, and serve the soup garnished with the green scallion parts and a drizzle of toasted sesame oil.

HEALTHY HOT AND SOUR SOUP

ACTIVE TIME: 30 TO 35 MINUTES | SERVES 8 AS AN APPETIZER

PORK:

⅔ pound pork tenderloin

2 tablespoons coconut aminos

1 tablespoon toasted sesame oil

Pinch of ground white pepper (optional)

SOUP:

2 tablespoons avocado oil

5 garlic cloves, thinly sliced

2 tablespoons finely chopped fresh ginger

6 scallions, chopped and separated into white and green parts

Salt

2 to 2½ cups finely sliced carrot (cut into matchsticks)

8 ounces fresh shiitake mushrooms, sliced

2 to 2½ cups chicken stock

1 tablespoon coconut aminos

Hot red pepper sauce (such as A&B American-Style Pepper Sauce) (optional)

2 tablespoons cider vinegar (or rice vinegar for milder taste)

2 large eggs (see note on following page)

1½ tablespoons arrowroot or tapioca starch

Pinch of ground white pepper (optional)

When I was growing up in Taiwan, my mom's hot and sour soup was always a dinner staple. It reminds me of family time with my parents and my brother. Unfortunately, the takeout restaurant version is filled with cornstarch and lacks the colorful vegetables and savory and sweet aroma that make the homemade version so special. Here I share a much healthier and way tastier version inspired by my mom's recipe.

1. PREPARE THE PORK: Slice the pork tenderloin into thin strips, place in a bowl, and season with the remaining pork ingredients. Mix well and set aside in the refrigerator.

2. PREPARE THE SOUP: Heat a heavy-bottomed soup pot or Dutch oven over medium-high heat, then add the avocado oil. Sauté the garlic, ginger, and white scallion parts until fragrant, about 10 seconds. Season with a pinch of salt. Add the seasoned pork. Season with another pinch of salt and sauté until the pork is no longer pink. Add the sliced carrot and shiitake mushrooms. Season with another pinch of salt and sauté for about 1 minute.

3. Add the chicken stock, cover, and bring to a simmer over medium heat. Season with the coconut aminos, hot pepper sauce to taste, if using, and cider vinegar. Give it a gentle stir, then adjust the seasoning to taste (perhaps more coconut aminos, vinegar, salt, white pepper, or hot sauce). Bring the soup to a boil and cook for 2 to 3 minutes.

4. Meanwhile, as the soup comes to a boil, whisk the eggs in a bowl. When the broth is boiling, turn off the heat. Hold chopsticks or a fork against one side of the bowl. From that side, slowly drizzle the eggs into the boiling soup in a swirling motion. Let the eggs stand for a few seconds to

continued

take shape in the boiling soup, and then gently whisk the broth and eggs to finish cooking.

5. Prepare a slurry of the arrowroot starch and 3 tablespoons cold water in a separate bowl. To thicken the soup, turn the heat back on and bring the soup to a simmer (not boiling). Give the arrowroot slurry another stir, then slowly drizzle it in. Gently whisk and let the broth simmer for about 1 minute, then turn off the heat. (If the slurry is overheated, the texture will break down.) Garnish with the green scallion parts and a pinch of white pepper, if desired. Serve hot and immediately.

Note

To form fluffy eggs, the broth needs to come to a rolling boil. If the temperature of the broth is not hot enough, it will not form fluffy eggs. If you can't have eggs, skip this step and thicken the soup with only the arrowroot slurry (see step 5).

SICHUAN DRY-FRIED GREEN BEANS WITH CRISPY PORK

ACTIVE TIME: 30 TO 35 MINUTES | SERVES 3

1½ tablespoons coconut aminos

2 teaspoons fish sauce (Red Boat brand preferred)

½ to 1 teaspoon harissa chili paste (Entube brand preferred) or tomato paste (for a nonspicy version)

1 pound string beans, trimmed, patted dry, and sliced into 2-inch pieces (see notes on following page)

3 tablespoons avocado oil

2 large garlic cloves, finely chopped

1 tablespoon finely chopped fresh ginger (or use 1½ tablespoons for a stronger flavor)

2 to 3 scallions, finely chopped and separated into white and green parts

4 to 5 Chinese dried red chiles (optional)

Salt

⅓ to ¼ pound ground pork, chicken, or turkey (see notes on following page)

This dish uses a simple contemporary Chinese cooking technique, dry-frying, to re-create the texture of blistered green beans without oily deep-frying (see notes). Traditional Chinese chili bean paste is replaced here by harissa chili paste to replicate that slightly spicy and complex, deep flavor. (Refer to page 17 for more information on this chili paste. It's a wonderful seasoning to keep in the pantry.) You can also use ground chicken or turkey, instead of pork, in this recipe. Serve with cauliflower rice, zoodles (zucchini noodles), or mixed greens.

1. To prepare the stir-fry sauce, combine the coconut aminos, fish sauce, and harissa in a small bowl and mix well. Set aside.

2. Heat a dry, large, stainless-steel skillet over medium-low heat until the skillet is almost at the smoking point. Add the green beans. Increase the heat to medium and stir-fry (this is called dry-fry in Chinese cooking) for 4 to 5 minutes, or until the beans are slightly blistered but not burnt.

3. Add 2 tablespoons of the avocado oil to the skillet and keep stir-frying the green beans for 2 to 3 more minutes. Remove from the skillet and set aside.

4. While the skillet is still hot, add the remaining tablespoon of avocado oil to the pan along with the garlic, ginger, white scallion parts, and red chiles. Season with a small pinch of salt and sauté until fragrant, 8 to 10 seconds. Add the

continued

ground pork. Season with another small pinch of salt. Sauté until the pork is completely cooked through, breaking it up into finer pieces.

5. Add 1 tablespoon of the stir-fry sauce to the ground pork. Stir-fry for 5 to 10 seconds, then add the green beans back to the skillet. Toss to coat everything well. Taste to see whether ½ to 1 more tablespoon of stir-fry sauce is needed.

6. Turn off the heat and stir in the green scallion parts. Serve hot and immediately.

Notes

In restaurants, the beans are quickly deep-fried to remove water content and attain a slightly crunchy and blistered texture. Here, a well-heated but oil-free skillet (preferably stainless steel) is crucial in re-creating the slightly blistered texture. Briskly stir-frying the green beans during the dry-fry process, making sure each bean has a chance to be in contact with the hot surface, is the key to achieving the right texture.

Green beans are the star of this dish. To keep them from becoming soggy, pay attention to the meat-to-bean ratio. Too much meat will result in more liquid in the sauté pan, changing the texture and making the dish less tasty.

LIFE-CHANGING CREAMY CHICKEN AND SHIITAKE CASSEROLE

ACTIVE TIME: 10 MINUTES | BAKE TIME: 25 TO 30 MINUTES | SERVES 3 TO 4

1 pound thinly sliced chicken breasts (see notes)

Your favorite chicken seasonings (mine are salt, pepper, garlic powder, red pepper flakes, and dried thyme or dill)

Ghee or avocado oil

1 large shallot, sliced into thin strips

4 to 5 garlic cloves, sliced

Salt

½ cup full-fat coconut milk, stirred well (see notes)

3 tablespoons chicken stock (see notes)

5 ounces fresh shiitake mushrooms, sliced

Nutritional yeast

This is my take on the Italian American classic chicken Marsala. Shiitake mushrooms add extra umami and a bit of Japanese flavor to this super flavorful, creamy, and easy chicken casserole. The chicken is half poached, half baked in a dairy-free cream. It will become one of your go-to chicken dishes! Serve with a simple salad and roasted potatoes for a complete meal.

1. Preheat the oven to 400°F.

2. Season the chicken with your favorite chicken seasonings. Heat a little ghee in a large skillet over medium-high heat. Quickly sear both sides of the chicken breasts to give them a nice golden brown sear on the outside. Transfer to a large casserole dish.

3. Heat additional ghee in the same skillet used for the chicken and sauté the shallot and garlic until fragrant. Season with a little salt to bring out the flavor. Layer the shallot and garlic over the chicken. Add the coconut milk and chicken stock. Spread the mushrooms over the chicken. Sprinkle with nutritional yeast.

4. Bake for 20 minutes, then increase the heat to 425°F for an additional 5 to 8 minutes, until the chicken is golden brown.

5. Sprinkle with more nutritional yeast before serving.

Notes

Can't find thinly sliced chicken breasts? Butterfly the breasts and lightly pound them to about ¼ inch thick.

When adding the coconut milk and chicken stock, adjust the quantity based on the size of the dish. Add just enough liquid to lightly touch the chicken breasts, not submerge them. For a thicker sauce to serve as a gravy, scoop a few tablespoons of the juices from the casserole dish after baking and thicken over low heat with a little arrowroot or tapioca starch.

PALEO CHICKEN KATSU

ACTIVE TIME: 25 TO 30 MINUTES | SERVES 4

½ green cabbage

1¼ to 1½ pounds thinly cut skinless, boneless chicken breasts or thighs

Coarse sea salt and freshly ground black pepper

¼ cup arrowroot starch or sweet potato flour

2 large eggs (see note)

6 tablespoons unsweetened shredded coconut

⅓ cup almond flour, or ¼ cup cassava flour

1½ tablespoons ghee

¼ cup I Heart Umami Sesame Ginger Sauce (page 189), chilled

Cauliflower rice, to serve

A healthier, lighter way to enjoy your favorite Japanese-inspired chicken katsu, *this version is made with almond flour and panfried to a golden crisp, then paired with shredded cabbage and Asian sesame ginger vinaigrette for a savory and satisfying meal!*

1. Slice the cabbage half into four wedges. Use a mandoline to thinly slice each wedge into long, thin shreds. Submerge the cabbage in ice-cold water. Set aside in the refrigerator.

2. If the chicken breast is thick, butterfly it: Place the chicken on a cutting board and, with your hand flat on top of it, use a sharp knife to slice horizontally through the breast, starting at the thickest section. Pound the pieces to an even thickness (about ¼ inch thick), using the bottom of a wide jar. Lightly season both sides with salt and pepper.

3. Prepare three large, shallow dishes: one with arrowroot starch; one with the eggs whisked with 2 to 3 tablespoons water; and one with the shredded coconut and almond flour well mixed. Season each with a little salt.

4. Heat the ghee in a large skillet over medium-high heat, then lower the heat to medium. Lightly coat the chicken with the arrowroot and shake off the excess. Dip the chicken into the egg, then coat it with the coconut mixture. Press to make sure the coconut sticks well to the chicken. Increase the heat to medium-high and panfry the chicken until both sides are golden brown, then lower the heat to medium and continue to cook for a few more minutes, or until the chicken is completely cooked through, flipping the breast often and watching it carefully to prevent burning. Set aside on a cooling rack.

5. Carefully slice the cutlets and serve immediately with the shredded cabbage (drain well before serving), sesame ginger dressing, and cauliflower rice.

Note

To prepare without egg, replace the egg batter with olive oil and a bit of fresh lemon juice.

HEALTHY TERIYAKI CHICKEN

ACTIVE TIME: 5 TO 10 MINUTES | BAKE TIME: 20 TO 25 MINUTES | SERVES 4

Cooking oil spray (avocado, coconut, or ghee)

4 boneless chicken thighs, skin on (about 1½ pounds)

Sea salt

⅓ cup I Heart Umami Teriyaki Sauce (page 187)

Toasted white sesame seeds (optional)

Chopped scallions (optional)

This chicken is made with no added sugar or starch and roasted in the oven with simplified cooking methods to help you enjoy good food fast. I highly recommend using boneless chicken thighs with the skin on. You can ask the butcher to remove the thigh bones for you, to save time! Serve with fresh leafy greens of your choice or with mashed potatoes or cauliflower rice.

1. Preheat the oven to 425°F. Line a sheet pan with parchment paper and place a baking rack on top. Lightly spray the rack with oil.

2. Pat the chicken dry. Lightly season with a bit of sea salt on all sides.

3. Place the chicken thighs, skin side up, on the prepared rack. Bake for 20 minutes, or until the skin becomes light golden brown and the meat is completely cooked through (165°F on a meat thermometer).

4. Remove the chicken from the oven and brush with the teriyaki sauce. Change the oven setting to HIGH BROIL. Place the chicken back in the oven and broil for 3 minutes to give the skin a nice golden color. (If you use skinless chicken, broil for only 1 to 2 minutes.)

5. Wait for 5 minutes before slicing the chicken into bite-sized pieces. If desired, sprinkle with toasted sesame seeds and chopped scallions.

CRISPY TURMERIC CHICKEN BAKE WITH LEEK

ACTIVE TIME: 15 MINUTES | BAKE TIME: ABOUT 50 MINUTES | SERVES 4

4 skin-on, bone-in chicken thighs (1⅔ pounds)

1 teaspoon ground turmeric or curry powder

½ teaspoon garlic powder

2 teaspoons coarse salt

½ teaspoon freshly ground black pepper

2 tablespoons ghee or avocado oil

1 large leek

1 Fresno or serrano chile, seeded and thinly sliced into strips (optional)

DAIRY-FREE TURMERIC CREAM:

About 1½ cups full-fat coconut milk

1 teaspoon ground turmeric or curry powder

2 tablespoons coconut aminos

Chicken thighs are baked in a creamy turmeric sauce until sweet and melt-in-your mouth tender. This simple, flavorful, hands-off dish will become your favorite chicken thigh casserole recipe! Serve with a bowl of fresh leafy green salad (my favorite is wild arugula mixed with romaine lettuce).

1. Preheat the oven to 375°F.

2. Season the chicken thighs—both the skin and the meaty sides—with the turmeric, garlic powder, salt, and pepper. Use your hands to gently rub in the spices so that the chicken will be more flavorful.

3. Heat a large cast-iron or stainless-steel skillet over medium to medium-low heat, heat the ghee, and place the chicken in the pan, skin side down. Crisp the skin without moving the chicken, 7 to 8 minutes. Once the skin is crispy, sear the flip side of the thighs for about 3 more minutes.

4. Meanwhile, cut off the tougher dark green part of the leek (save it to use in soup stock). Dice the remainder of the leek into rounds: the white parts about ¼ inch thick and the green parts to a little less than ¼ inch thick. Separate the white and green parts. Rinse under cold water until clean. Drain and set aside.

5. Stir all the turmeric cream ingredients together in a small bowl.

6. Place the green leek parts in the bottom of a casserole dish. Pour in the turmeric cream (see note on page 44), evenly distributing it in the casserole dish. Place the seared chicken thighs, skin side up, on top of the leek. Pour in any

continued

extra chicken juices from the skillet. Gently wiggle and push the chicken down a bit so that the meaty bottom parts touch the cream and the skin is above the cream (i.e., not touching the cream). Place the white leek parts around and between the chicken thighs. Arrange the chile slices, if using, on top of the chicken.

7. Bake for 40 minutes, then increase the temperature to 400°F and bake for 8 to 10 more minutes, or until a meat thermometer reaches 165°F at the thickest part of the chicken. Remove the dish from the oven. Let cool for 10 to 15 minutes. The sauce will thicken further.

Note

My casserole dish is an 8½-by-13-inch oval, but chances are your casserole dish will be a different size than mine. Use a dish that's just about the right size to fit in all the chicken thighs with a small amount of space in between. How much turmeric cream should you add to the dish? A good rule of thumb: you want to add just enough turmeric cream that it touches the bottom, meaty side of the chicken yet not too much that it will spill over or cover the crispy skin. If your casserole dish is smaller than mine, use less turmeric cream, and vice versa.

THAI-INSPIRED PALEO SALMON CAKES

ACTIVE TIME: 30 TO 35 MINUTES | SERVES 3

DAIRY-FREE AIOLI:

¼ cup fresh lemon juice

1 garlic clove, grated

1 teaspoon I Heart Umami Paleo Worcestershire Sauce (page 188)

¼ teaspoon coarse salt

¼ teaspoon freshly ground black pepper

1 tablespoon Dijon mustard

3 heaping tablespoons nutritional yeast

½ cup olive oil

SALMON CAKES:

1 tablespoon ground flaxseed meal or ground chia seeds (or substitute 1 large egg; see directions)

½ shallot

¼ cup fresh parsley or cilantro

¼ cup finely chopped carrot

Zest and juice of ½ lime

3 teaspoons red curry paste (Thai Kitchen brand preferred)

½ teaspoon coarse salt

½ cup frozen spinach, defrosted and squeezed of excess liquid (optional)

1 to 1¼ pounds skinless, boneless wild-caught salmon

¼ teaspoon garlic powder

¼ teaspoon onion powder

Pinch of red chili powder (optional)

Avocado oil

These super flavorful salmon cakes are fragrant with red curry paste. The aioli dressing is made without eggs, mayonnaise, flour, or starch. This is a perfect recipe for people who are allergic to eggs or want a lighter and more refreshing dish. Serve on a bed of mixed leafy greens.

1. MAKE THE AIOLI: Combine all the aioli ingredients, except the olive oil, in a small bowl. Slowly stream in the olive oil, whisking, until the dressing is emulsified. Cover and set aside in the refrigerator.

2. PREPARE THE SALMON CAKES: Mix the flaxseed meal and 3 tablespoons water in a small bowl. Set aside for 20 to 30 minutes while preparing the other ingredients. (If using an egg instead of the flaxseed mixture, set it aside until step 5.)

3. Place the shallot, parsley, carrot, lime juice and zest, curry paste, salt, and spinach in a food processor and pulse until the carrot is finely chopped. Remove from the food processor and set aside.

4. Place the salmon in the same food processor bowl (no need to rinse) and mince into small pieces, retaining a chunky texture.

5. Place the chopped salmon, shallot mixture, garlic powder, onion powder, chili powder, and flax mixture (or egg, if using instead of the flaxseed mixture) in a large bowl. Use your hands to thoroughly combine. The mixture will be loose at first, but after a few minutes it will bind together.

6. FORM THE CAKES: Line a large baking sheet with parchment paper. Using a ¼-cup measuring cup, scoop the mixture and place on the prepared pan. Grease your hands

continued

with avocado oil, then delicately form the balls into patties (see note).

7. Heat a large skillet over medium heat. Add 2 to 3 tablespoons of avocado oil and allow the oil to heat before adding the patties. Add them in batches so as not to overcrowd the skillet. Cook for about 3 minutes, then carefully and gently flip, using a spatula. Cook for an additional 3 minutes for well done. (Cooking the patties for 2 minutes per side will yield a medium-rare center.)

8. Serve on a bed of mixed leafy greens and drizzle the aioli over the greens and salmon cakes.

Note

To avoid a mess when forming the salmon cakes, I set a clean paper towel next to my oil bottle so when I need more oil to grease my palms, I can use the paper towel to hold the bottle.

SILKY EGG STIR-FRY WITH JUMBO SHRIMP

ACTIVE TIME: 15 MINUTES | SERVES 2

12 medium raw shrimp (about ½ pound), peeled and deveined

6 large eggs

½ teaspoon coarse sea salt, plus a pinch

⅛ teaspoon ground white pepper

5 to 6 tablespoons chopped scallions (or more if you like)

1 teaspoon arrowroot starch

1½ tablespoons ghee

2 medium firm (not ripe) tomatoes, roughly chopped

2 tablespoons tomato paste

Toasted sesame oil for serving

This dish is very popular in Hong Kong, Taiwan, and China because it's super fast to make and tastes delicious. It could also be made without shrimp for a simple silky egg and tomato stir-fry. Serve with cauliflower rice or Simple Cauli Fried Rice (page 162).

1. Blanch the shrimp by bringing a pot of water to a boil, then add the shrimp. As soon as the shrimp turn pink and start curling up, scoop them out and drain. Set aside.

2. Place the eggs, ½ teaspoon of salt, the white pepper, and 2 tablespoons of chopped scallions in a medium bowl. In a separate bowl, whisk the arrowroot starch with a little less than 1 tablespoon water and add to the egg mixture and gently whisk. Add the shrimp to the egg mixture.

3. Heat a large skillet over medium-high heat, add 1 tablespoon of the ghee, and lower the heat to medium. Add the shrimp and egg mixture. Gently stir-fry until the eggs are about 70 percent cooked, similar to soft, runny scrambled eggs. Scoop the mixture out of the pan and set aside.

4. Add the remaining ½ tablespoon of ghee to the skillet, then add the remaining 3 to 4 tablespoons of scallions, the chopped tomato, and the tomato paste. Season with a small pinch of salt. Sauté for about 10 seconds. Add the shrimp and eggs back to the pan and give a quick toss, about 5 seconds.

5. Serve hot with cauliflower rice. Drizzle with sesame oil and top with more scallions, if desired.

DAN DAN SESAME NOODLES

ACTIVE TIME: 25 MINUTES | SERVES 2

PORK:

½ to ¾ pound ground pork, chicken, or turkey

1 tablespoon coconut aminos

1½ teaspoons toasted sesame oil

DAN DAN SAUCE:

2 tablespoons tahini

1½ tablespoons cashew butter

2 tablespoons coconut aminos

1 tablespoon aged balsamic vinegar

1 fat garlic clove, grated or crushed (use 2 cloves for a stronger flavor)

1 tablespoon toasted or hot sesame oil

¼ teaspoon ground cumin

⅛ teaspoon Chinese five-spice powder

3 tablespoons chicken or vegetable stock or water (add more liquid for a thinner sauce)

STIR-FRY:

2 tablespoons avocado oil

2 garlic cloves, finely chopped

2 to 3 scallions, chopped and separated into white and green parts

1½ teaspoons finely chopped fresh ginger

This dish is inspired by my childhood favorite noodle shop in Taiwan. Dan Dan noodles originally came from China, and the optional pickles and ground Sichuan peppercorns in my recipe mimic the flavor of that version. The version made in Taiwan (and Japan) tastes lighter and slightly sweeter. This is an easy and deeply satisfying dish that you and your family can enjoy throughout the year.

1. MARINATE THE PORK: Place the ground pork in a bowl with the coconut aminos and sesame oil. Mix well and set aside in the refrigerator for 10 to 15 minutes.

2. MAKE THE SAUCE: Combine all the Dan Dan sauce ingredients in a small bowl, mix well, and set aside.

3. BEGIN THE STIR-FRY: Heat a large skillet or wok over medium-high heat, then lower the heat to medium. Add the avocado oil and swirl the oil around the skillet. Add the garlic, white scallion parts, ginger, and ground Sichuan pepper. Season with a small pinch of salt and lightly sauté until fragrant, 8 to 10 seconds. Add the marinated ground pork. Keep sautéing until the pork breaks up further into finer pieces, 10 to 12 minutes.

4. Add the chopped pickles, if using, and coconut aminos. Sauté over medium heat until the moisture has evaporated and the ground pork becomes crisp but not burnt, similar to the texture of fried bacon bits. Turn off the heat. Mix in a handful of green scallion parts (reserve some for topping). Set aside.

1 teaspoon Sichuan peppercorns, ground, or ¼ teaspoon freshly ground black pepper mixed with 2 teaspoons lemon zest (optional)

Salt

1 to 1½ tablespoons chopped pickles (such as Bubbies Kosher Dill; optional)

1 tablespoon coconut aminos

TO ASSEMBLE:

1 large or 2 medium zucchini, spiralized

Almond slices, roughly chopped (optional)

Red chiles (Fresno or serrano), thinly sliced (optional), for garnish

5. To assemble, divide the Dan Dan sauce between two large bowls. Divide the zucchini noodles between the bowls, top each bowl with 2 to 3 tablespoons of crispy ground pork, chopped almonds, and green scallion parts. Drizzle with a bit more sesame oil, if you like. Mix everything together and serve immediately.

BEEF AND BROCCOLI

ACTIVE TIME: 20 MINUTES | SERVES 4

ASIAN PALEO

BEEF:

1 pound beef sirloin or skirt steak

2 tablespoons coconut aminos

½ teaspoon coarse sea salt

2 to 3 teaspoons toasted sesame oil

¼ teaspoon freshly ground black pepper

1 teaspoon arrowroot starch

½ teaspoon baking soda

STIR-FRY SAUCE:

2 tablespoons coconut aminos

1 tablespoon fish sauce (Red Boat brand preferred)

2 teaspoons toasted sesame oil

¼ teaspoon freshly ground black pepper

ADDITIONAL STIR-FRY INGREDIENTS:

1 to 2 heads broccoli, broken into florets

1½ tablespoons ghee

2 garlic cloves, minced

2 thin slices ginger, finely chopped (about 1½ tablespoons)

Chopped green scallion for garnish

This recipe is by far the most popular dish on my website and there's a reason that this dish has become people's favorite: it's easy, super flavorful, and you can easily swap in chicken and/or shrimp. Beef and broccoli is a Chinese American staple. I first tried it when I moved to the United States, and it reminded me of a beef stir-fry dish made with oyster sauce and Chinese broccoli in Taiwan. When I decided to make my version, I followed my taste buds and made it lighter and healthier, with less starch and no added sugar. Serve it with Simple Cauli Fried Rice (page 162), any mixed leafy green salad, or mashed sweet potatoes for a complete meal.

1. MARINATE THE BEEF: Slice the beef against the grain to about ¼ inch thick and place in a bowl. Add the remaining beef ingredients. Mix well and set aside in the refrigerator.

2. PREPARE THE STIR-FRY SAUCE: Combine the coconut aminos, fish sauce, toasted sesame oil, and black pepper in a small bowl and mix well. Set aside.

3. Blanch the broccoli florets in boiling water for 1 to 2 minutes. Soak in cold water to stop the cooking, then drain.

4. Heat the ghee in a sauté pan over medium-high heat, then lower the heat to medium and add the garlic and ginger. Season with a small pinch of salt and stir-fry until fragrant, 8 to 10 seconds. Be careful not to burn the aromatics.

5. Increase the heat to medium-high and add the marinated beef. Spread the beef evenly over the bottom of the skillet and cook until the edges of the beef are slightly charred and crispy. Do the same thing for the flip side, cooking three-quarters of the way through.

6. Add the stir-fry sauce and stir-fry for about 1 minute.

7. Add the blanched broccoli. Stir-fry for another 30 seconds, tossing to combine. Serve hot and immediately.

THAI GRILLED STEAK SALAD

ACTIVE TIME: 25 MINUTES | SERVES 3

BEEF:

1 pound beef sirloin or skirt steak

Sea salt and freshly ground black pepper

2 teaspoons ghee

DRESSING:

3 small garlic cloves, crushed

1 red chile (Fresno, serrano, or Thai), seeded and finely chopped

2 tablespoons coconut aminos

1 tablespoon fish sauce (Red Boat brand preferred)

2 teaspoons red chili sauce

2 to 3 tablespoons fresh lime juice

SALAD:

2 small seedless cucumbers, sliced

1 shallot, thinly sliced

Handful of fresh cilantro, roughly chopped

Handful of mixed greens

Cherry tomatoes, sliced

My husband loves a good bowl of steak salad. For this version, I made a wonderful Thai-inspired salad dressing. I slightly warm up the dressing to bring out deeper aromatic flavor and that balances with the savory steak and fresh leafy greens for a hearty and healthy everyday go-to meal.

1. PREPARE THE BEEF: Season the beef with salt and black pepper. Heat the ghee in a grill pan over high heat, then grill the steak for 2 to 3 minutes per side for medium or medium-rare, or until your desired doneness. Set the steak aside to rest and cover with aluminum foil.

2. MAKE THE DRESSING: Combine all the dressing ingredients, except the lime juice, in a small saucepan. Slightly warm the dressing over low heat for 2 to 3 minutes, using a wooden spoon to gently stir. Stir in 2 tablespoons of the lime juice. Turn off the heat. Pour the dressing into a bowl and set aside.

3. ASSEMBLE THE SALAD: Mix together the cucumber, shallot, cilantro, mixed greens, and tomatoes in a large salad bowl. Thinly slice the beef against the grain and add to the bowl.

4. Pour the dressing over the beef and greens. Toss to combine. Wait for 1 to 2 minutes, taste, and add up to 1 more tablespoon of lime juice if desired. Serve warm and immediately.

MONGOLIAN BEEF

ACTIVE TIME: 20 MINUTES | SERVES 4

BEEF:

1 pound beef sirloin tips, sirloin steak, or skirt steak

2 tablespoons coconut aminos

1 tablespoon fish sauce (Red Boat brand preferred)

2 teaspoons toasted sesame oil

STIR-FRY:

Ghee, avocado oil, or coconut oil

3 large garlic cloves, finely minced

One 3-inch piece fresh ginger, thinly sliced into long, thin strips

2 red Fresno or serrano red chiles, seeded and sliced into long, thin strips (optional)

3 scallions, cut into 3-inch lengths and separated into white and green parts

Salt

3 to 4 large handfuls mixed greens of your choice

Mongolian Beef is the English translation of cōng bào niúròu *in Mandarin. It literally means "beef with scallion and ginger stir-fry." This Paleo version is full of flavor, using Asian aromatics and quick stir-fries in a well-heated skillet. It's full of flavor, color, and texture.*

1. MARINATE THE BEEF: Thinly slice the beef against the grain, ⅛ to ¼ inch thick. Place in a bowl with the remaining beef ingredients. Marinate the beef in the refrigerator for 15 to 20 minutes.

2. BEGIN THE STIR-FRY: Heat 1 tablespoon of ghee over medium-high heat in a large skillet or sauté pan, then lower the heat to medium. Stir-fry the beef with its marinade until the meat is no longer pink. Transfer to a bowl along with the juices in the skillet and set aside.

3. Add a bit more ghee to the skillet and sauté the garlic, ginger, red chiles, and white scallion parts over medium to medium-high heat until fragrant. Season with a small pinch of salt. Add the beef back to the pan along with the green scallion parts. Toss everything to combine.

4. Serve the beef over a handful of your favorite mixed greens. You should have some liquid left in the pan. Use that delicious sauce as a dressing.

WEEK

BATCH COOK

WEEKEND

EASY

FLAVOR

NIGHT BFF

ING PERFECT

FUN

ADD-ONS

POP

Batch cooking is the key to healthy and fresh homemade meals. Setting time aside to prepare a few meals during the weekend can help alleviate stress and reduce the time you spend wondering what to eat tonight. Many of the readers of my blog tell me that these recipes have become their weekly meal rotation for their family and have helped them cut down on the need to order takeout!

If batch cooking is new to you, start with one dish from this section and follow the meal planning notes. You'll come home to healthy savory meals in no time! For more batch cooking and weekly meal planning ideas, see page 192.

VEGAN TANDOORI CAULIFLOWER AND KALE BREAKFAST HASH

ACTIVE TIME: 15 MINUTES | BAKE TIME: 25 MINUTES | SERVES 4

1 large head cauliflower, roughly chopped

1 large shallot, sliced into strips

1 red bell pepper, roughly diced

¼ cup olive oil

½ teaspoon coarse salt

¼ teaspoon freshly ground black pepper

4 to 5 tablespoons store-bought tandoori masala seasoning

1 large bunch kale leaves, stemmed and roughly chopped

1 tablespoon avocado oil

Dash of fresh lemon juice

Leftover baked sweet potatoes, diced (optional)

This plant-based recipe is quick to make and you can replace the tandoori spices with any other dried spices that you like. It is also wonderful as a side dish. Feel free to go nonvegan and add an egg, grilled chicken, or steak for extra protein.

1. Preheat the oven to 400°F. Line a large baking sheet (you may need two sheets) with parchment paper.

2. Toss the cauliflower, shallot, and bell pepper with the olive oil on the prepared pan and season with salt and black pepper. Sprinkle generously with the tandoori masala seasoning. Bake for 25 to 30 minutes.

3. In the meantime, sauté the kale leaves in avocado oil until the leaves have withered a bit. Season with a little salt and a dash of lemon juice. (Too much lemon juice will make it sour, so taste and adjust.)

4. In a bowl, combine the kale, roasted veggies, and baked sweet potato, if using. Serve hot or at room temperature.

ELECTRIC PRESSURE COOKER CHINESE CHICKEN BONE BROTH

ACTIVE TIME: 10 MINUTES | PRESSURE COOKER TIME: 30 MINUTES | SERVES 8

1 packet Root and Spring brand Health and Immunity Chinese herbal soup mix (see page 20)

One 3- to 3¾-pound whole chicken, skin on and bone in (giblets removed)

3 to 4 cups cubed carrot

2½ cups peeled and cubed daikon (Chinese radish) (optional)

1 cup rehydrated shiitake mushrooms, sliced (rehydrate the mushrooms overnight and keep the mushroom water; optional)

Coarse sea salt

Bok choy or baby spinach (optional)

This simple bone broth recipe is easy and quick to make in an electric pressure cooker. You can also make it on the stovetop or in a slow cooker. This soup will nourish your body and keep you healthy throughout the year! Serve with veggies, such as the Quick Garlic-Ginger Kale Sauté (page 165) and a good carb, such as the Easy Roasted Cinnamon Butternut Squash (page 172).

1. Lightly rinse the Chinese herbs under cool running water. Place the herbs and chicken in a 6-quart electric pressure cooker. Add the carrot, daikon, rehydrated shiitake mushrooms, and mushroom water, if using. Fill the pot with enough water to just cover the entire chicken, 8 to 10 cups. The pressure cooker should not be more than two-thirds full.

2. Seal the pressure cooker valve and set for high pressure for 30 minutes. Allow it to come to natural pressure release. To cook in a slow cooker: Cook on LOW for 8 to 10 hours or up to 24 hours, depending on the richness of the herbal flavor you prefer. To cook on the stovetop: Bring the ingredients to a boil in a soup pot, then lower the heat and simmer for 1½ to 2 hours. You may need to add a bit more water to compensate for evaporation.

3. After the pressure releases, season with coarse sea salt to taste. Strain before serving (the herb flavor will become stronger once the soup cools; see note). You may also remove the chicken and shred the meat and then add it back to the soup pot.

4. Serve with Easy Roasted Cinnamon Butternut Squash (page 172; leave the skin on and slice the squash into half-rings for a prettier presentation) and a handful of leafy greens, such as bok choy or baby spinach.

Note

The herbal flavor will become richer the longer you cook the herbs. I usually leave the herbs in the pot and reheat the entire broth again with the herbs the next day. The broth will become darker with a stronger herb flavor. However, if this is your first time trying a Chinese herbal soup mix, you can strain out the herbs. Store them in a glass container in the refrigerator. If you decide for an herbier flavor the next day, reheat them with the broth. Discard the cooked herbs if not using them after 3 days.

TURMERIC-GINGER KABOCHA SQUASH SOUP

ACTIVE TIME: 20 MINUTES | COOK TIME: 20 MINUTES | SERVES 8 AS AN APPETIZER

SOUP:

1 medium kabocha squash

2 tablespoons ghee or avocado oil

1 large shallot, chopped

Coarse salt

Up to 2 cups chicken or vegetable stock

1 to 2 teaspoons ground turmeric, or more to taste

1 to 2 pinches Vietnamese cinnamon, or more to taste

½ cup full-fat coconut milk, stirred well, or more if desired

1 to 2 teaspoons grated frozen ginger (see note, page 165)

QUICK KALE SAUTÉ (OPTIONAL):

2 tablespoons avocado oil

1 large shallot, sliced into thin strips

Salt

1 large bunch curly kale, stemmed and roughly chopped

1 to 2 tablespoons chicken or vegetable stock or water

1 to 2 teaspoons extra virgin olive oil

I've always loved Japanese kabocha squash. Its sweet and earthy taste adds an extra flavor dimension when softened and mixed with coconut milk cream. The same cooking method can be applied for other types of squash. Enjoy a bowl of this lovely, healthy, and delicious soup on colder nights.

I intentionally left the seasoning measurements less precise in this recipe to allow you to make adjustments to your own liking. If you aren't sure, start with the minimums recommended in the recipe and add more if you like.

1. PREPARE THE SOUP: Use a sharp knife to cut the kabocha in half, slowly and carefully wiggling your knife in a rocking motion and avoiding cutting through the center stem. Slice each half into four quarters. Scoop out the seeds with a spoon and remove the skin with a knife. Dice the squash into bite-sized cubes.

2. Heat the ghee in a large (6-quart) Dutch oven or heavy soup pot over medium-high heat, then add the shallot. Season with a small pinch of salt and sauté until fragrant, 10 to 12 seconds. Add the diced kabocha and season with another pinch of salt. Sauté for a few more minutes. Add just enough stock to cover the squash. Add the turmeric and cinnamon. Give it a stir and cover with a lid. Cook over medium heat until the squash becomes soft, about 15 minutes.

3. MEANWHILE, PREPARE THE KALE, IF USING: Heat a large skillet over medium-high heat, then lower the heat to medium. Add the avocado oil and the shallot. Season

continued

with a small pinch of salt and sauté until fragrant. Add the chopped kale. Keep sautéing for a few more minutes. Add the stock and lower the heat to medium-low. Cover the skillet with a lid and allow the kale to cook for a few more minutes. Season with a bit more salt and drizzle with the olive oil.

4. Use an immersion blender (or scoop the squash into a regular blender) to blend the squash soup until creamy and smooth. Reheat over medium-low heat and add full-fat coconut milk to reach your desired consistency. Grate 1 teaspoon's worth of frozen ginger into the pot, give it a quick stir, and see whether you'd like to add more spices. Serve hot or slightly chilled, topped with the kale sauté or accompanied by any protein of your choice.

ELECTRIC PRESSURE COOKER AROMATIC CHICKEN AND SPARERIB SOUP

ACTIVE TIME: 10 TO 15 MINUTES | PRESSURE COOKER TIME: 50 MINUTES | SERVES 8

6 skin-on or skinless chicken drumsticks

1 pound baby spareribs

1¾ cups diced celery

1¾ cups diced carrot

4 ounces fresh shiitake mushrooms, sliced

1½ cups lotus root, peeled and diced (optional; see note on following page)

1 thumb-sized piece fresh ginger

Low-sodium chicken stock mixed with water

Sea salt

This soup is inspired by a Hong Kongese–style soup called jīnhuá huǒtuǐ jītāng—a special type of cured ham stewed with chicken in a clear broth. Since this particular ham can be difficult to find in the United States, I used spareribs instead. The chicken and the pork ribs are simmered in a light and savory broth until they're fall-off-the-bone tender. This combination adds an extra flavor complexity and is absolutely out-of-this-world delicious.

1. To make the best broth, fill a large pot with just enough water to cover the chicken and ribs. Bring the water alone to a boil, then add the chicken and ribs. Cook over high heat until the water returns to a boil and there is no blood coming out, 5 to 7 minutes after the water returns to a boil. Turn off the heat.

2. Discard the murky water. Rinse the chicken and ribs under room-temperature water that is slightly warm to the touch.

3. Place the cleaned chicken and ribs in an electric pressure cooker along with the rest of the ingredients, except the salt, adding enough water or chicken stock to cover (see following page). For slow cooker and stovetop instructions, see notes on following page.

4. Turn the valve to the sealing position. Press SOUP and set to 50 minutes. When the cooking time is finished, let it come to natural pressure release. The soup might burst through the valve if you use quick release.

5. Season with sea salt to taste before serving.

continued

Note

Lotus root is the root of the lotus flower, which is an aquatic plant. It is very common in Asian dishes. To prepare it for cooking, first cut off the tip end of the root, wash and peel off the outer skin with a vegetable peeler, then dice the root into smaller chunks or thinly slice. When added to soups, braises, or stews, the roots become sweet and tender. They are also great thinly sliced and added to stir-fries or chilled salad.

ALTERNATE COOKING METHODS

- To cook in a slow cooker: Follow steps 1 and 2. Place the cleaned chicken and ribs in a slow cooker along with the rest of the ingredients, except the salt, adding enough water or chicken stock to cover (see box). Cook on LOW for 8 to 10 hours. Season with sea salt to taste before serving.

- To cook on the stovetop: Follow steps 1 and 2. Place the cleaned chicken and ribs in a large pot along with the rest of the ingredients, except the salt, adding enough water or chicken stock to cover (see box). Place over low to medium-low heat and simmer for 2 hours. You may need to add a bit more stock or water to compensate for evaporation. Season with sea salt to taste before serving.

HOW MUCH LIQUID TO ADD TO THE SOUP POT?

- In an electric pressure cooker, the liquid level should be about 1 inch higher than the ingredients, always making sure not to exceed the maximum fill line indicated in the pressure cooker's inner pot. In general, you should only fill the pot two-thirds full, for safety.

- In a slow cooker, the liquid level should be about 1½ inches higher than the ingredients.

- And if you use a clay pot or a regular large soup pot to cook over a stovetop, you may need to add more water during the cooking process, to compensate for the water evaporation.

ELECTRIC PRESSURE COOKER BRISKET PHO

ACTIVE TIME: 20 TO 25 MINUTES | PRESSURE COOKER TIME: 40 MINUTES | SERVES: 8 PEOPLE

PHO:

1¼ cups dried shiitake mushrooms

1¾ to 2 pounds beef brisket

1 to 1¼ pounds beef shank soup bones, beef knuckle bones, or a combination

1 large leek, roughly diced into segments

3 carrots, roughly chopped

1 medium yellow onion, peeled but not sliced (leave whole)

2½ teaspoons fine sea salt

1 tablespoon fish sauce (Red Boat brand preferred)

1 teaspoon Chinese five-spice powder (optional)

PHO AROMATICS:

2 fat, thumb-sized pieces fresh ginger, scrubbed clean (no need to peel)

4 star anise

2 cinnamon sticks

8 green cardamom pods

3 medium shallots

4 to 5 cilantro sprigs or 1½ teaspoons coriander seeds

GARNISHES:

Bean sprouts

Red or green Fresno chiles

This dish is inspired by my favorite Vietnamese noodle shop in Bushwick, Brooklyn. It might take a bit of time to gather the ingredients, but the result is absolutely rewarding and delicious. Make a big pot and enjoy it throughout the week. The following ingredient measurements and cooking time are for a 6-quart electric pressure cooker. Make sure not to overfill the soup pot. You need to leave some space to allow the liquid to come to a boil without spilling over. (If your pressure cooker is smaller, see notes for how to reduce the quantity of the beef bones, carrots, and salt.)

TO PREPARE:

1. Soak the dried shiitake mushrooms overnight in room-temperature water. If rushed for time, soak in warm water until the mushrooms are soft and tender.

2. PREBOIL THE BRISKET AND BONES (SEE NOTES ON PAGE 75): Place the brisket and bones in a large stockpot and cover with water. Bring the water to a boil over high heat, and lower the heat to medium and simmer for 10 more minutes. Rinse the bones and meat under room-temperature tap water. Set aside. Discard the broth.

3. PREPARE THE AROMATICS: Toast the pho aromatics in a dry, cast-iron skillet over medium heat. Rotate and flip the ingredients frequently until you can smell a lovely fragrance. Be careful not to burn them (a slight char is okay).

4. Slice the rehydrated mushrooms and set aside. Reserve the mushroom water. Place the toasted aromatics and leek in large tea bags or a cheesecloth tied with string (see notes on page 75).

continued

Fresh mint leaves

Baby bok choy

Fresh Thai basil (optional)

Fresh cilantro (optional)

Hot chili sauce (optional)

Lime wedges

ELECTRIC PRESSURE COOKER COOKING:

1. Place the precooked brisket and beef bones (fatty side up), carrot, onion, and aromatics bundle in a 6-quart electric pressure cooker. Strain the mushroom water as you add the liquid to the pot. Top up with tap water until it reaches the 4-quart/liter mark. Close the lid in the sealing position, press SOUP, and set to 40 minutes/high pressure/more.

2. Allow the pressure cooker to come to natural pressure release.

3. Remove the brisket and soak it in cold water for at least 10 minutes, making sure that it is fully submerged. This will prevent the meat from turning a dark color. Discard the aromatics bundle, bones, and onion. Season the broth with the sea salt, fish sauce, and five-spice powder, if using.

4. Thinly slice the brisket against the grain at a 45-degree angle. Ladle the broth, brisket, and rehydrated mushrooms into bowls and add bean sprouts, chile peppers, mint leaves, baby bok choy, and your desired quantities of Thai basil, cilantro, and hot chili sauce, if using. Serve hot with lime wedges.

Notes

Preboiling the meat and bones is an important step to produce a clear pho broth. The boiling process will remove the blood and other small bone fragments or impurities.

Use tea or spice bags to hold the aromatics and leeks. It's an easier way to discard them after cooking. If using cheesecloth tied with a string, be sure the cloth is fine enough that the aroma flavor can come through.

If your electric pressure cooker is smaller than 6 quarts, reduce the beef bone and brisket quantity by ¼ to ½ pound and adjust the other ingredient quantities to 1 cup of dried shiitake mushrooms, 2 carrots, and 1½ teaspoons of fine sea salt (taste the cooked soup and see whether more salt is needed).

If you follow the directions, there's no need to strain the broth after cooking. However, you may do so, if desired.

KUNG PAO CHICKEN

ACTIVE TIME: 35 MINUTES | SERVES 3 TO 4

CHICKEN:

1½ pounds skinless, boneless chicken breasts or thighs

1½ tablespoons coconut aminos

¼ teaspoon garlic powder

¼ teaspoon onion powder

¼ teaspoon coarse salt

½ teaspoon arrowroot starch

2 to 3 tablespoons ghee or avocado oil

AROMATICS:

3 to 4 garlic cloves, sliced

2 thin slices fresh ginger, finely chopped (about 1 tablespoon)

2 to 3 scallions, chopped (reserve some green parts for serving)

1 red Fresno chile, seeded and finely chopped

5 Chinese dried red chiles

1 tablespoon Sichuan peppercorns (optional, or substitute ¼ teaspoon freshly ground black pepper plus 2 teaspoons lemon zest)

Salt

STIR-FRY SAUCE:

2 tablespoons coconut aminos

1 teaspoon rice or cider vinegar

1 teaspoon harissa chili paste (Entube brand preferred)

¼ teaspoon arrowroot starch

Toasted sesame oil (optional)

This dish is full of flavor and character and you'll notice that the aromatics add extra color and texture. Sichuan peppercorns can be found at your local Chinese grocery store or ordered online. They give the lemony flavor and numbing mouthfeel that make Kung Pao chicken so special. For a mild version, replace the peppers with one red bell pepper cut into bite-sized pieces and the harissa with tomato paste.

1. MARINATE THE CHICKEN: Chop the chicken into small bite-sized pieces, place in a medium bowl, and add the remaining chicken ingredients except the oil. Marinate for 10 to 15 minutes in the refrigerator.

2. Heat a large stainless-steel skillet over medium-high heat, then add 1 to 1½ tablespoons of the ghee. Add the marinated chicken. Panfry in one shallow layer so the chicken pieces become crisp and golden brown, cooking until about 75 percent cooked through, about 3 minutes on one side, and flip and cook for 1 to 2 minutes on the other side. Remove from the pan and set aside.

3. PREPARE THE AROMATICS: While the skillet is still hot, add 1 to 1½ tablespoons more ghee. Add the aromatics. Season with a small pinch of salt and sauté until fragrant, 8 to 10 seconds.

4. PREPARE THE STIR-FRY SAUCE: In a small bowl, mix together the sauce ingredients and then add the sauce to the skillet. Quickly stir-fry and coat the aromatics with the sauce, then add the chicken back to the skillet. Coat the chicken with the sauce and keep stir-frying until the chicken is completely cooked through.

5. Serve hot and immediately with chopped green scallions and a few teaspoons of sesame oil, if desired.

MEAL-PLANNING

Thinly slice and marinate the chicken. Store in the refrigerator if using the next day, or otherwise in the freezer. Defrost overnight in the refrigerator before cooking.

SWEET-AND-SOUR CHICKEN

ACTIVE TIME: 30 TO 35 MINUTES | SERVES 4

CHICKEN:

1¼ pounds skinless, boneless chicken breasts or thighs

1¼ teaspoons coarse sea salt

1½ tablespoons coconut aminos

¼ teaspoon ground white pepper

½ teaspoon ground ginger

1 large egg white, lightly beaten

1 tablespoon toasted sesame oil

2 teaspoons arrowroot starch

STIR-FRY:

3½ tablespoons avocado oil or ghee

¼ yellow onion, diced

1 scallion, chopped

2 or 3 thin slices ginger, roughly chopped

Salt

½ green bell pepper, cut into bite-sized cubes

½ red bell pepper, cut into bite-sized cubes

3 to 4 tablespoons I Heart Umami Sweet-and-Sour Sauce (page 185)

This is one of my readers' favorite recipes. I use dried apricots to sweeten the sauce naturally and balance the sweetness with rice vinegar and tomato paste to give it a nice tart and sweet flavor. It tastes much better and is healthier than any takeout!

1. MARINATE THE CHICKEN: Thinly slice the chicken breasts or dice the chicken thighs. Mix well in a medium bowl with the remaining chicken ingredients. Marinate in the refrigerator while preparing the stir-fry ingredients.

2. START THE STIR-FRY: Heat 3 tablespoons of the avocado oil over medium-high heat in a large skillet, then lower the heat to medium. Carefully place the chicken in the skillet in one shallow layer and panfry until golden brown, flipping once to cook both sides. Set aside along with the chicken juice.

3. Heat the remaining 1½ teaspoons of oil over medium-high heat in the same skillet, then lower the heat to medium. Add the onion, scallion, and ginger. Season with a small pinch of salt. Stir-fry for 5 to 10 seconds. Add the bell peppers. Season with another small pinch of salt and stir-fry for 5 to 10 seconds. Add the chicken back to the skillet. Add 3 to 4 heaping tablespoons of the sweet-and-sour sauce. Keep stir-frying until the chicken is completely cooked through. Serve hot and immediately.

MEAL-PLANNING

Thinly slice and marinate the chicken. Store in the refrigerator if using the next day, or otherwise in the freezer. Defrost overnight in the refrigerator before cooking.

CHINESE SESAME CHICKEN

ACTIVE TIME: 35 MINUTES | SERVES 4

CHICKEN:

1¼ pounds skinless, boneless chicken thighs and/or breasts

Salt and freshly ground black pepper

¼ teaspoon ground ginger

½ teaspoon arrowroot or tapioca starch

1 tablespoon olive oil

Avocado oil

STIR-FRY:

2 or 3 thin slices fresh ginger

1 large garlic clove, thinly sliced

3 to 4 tablespoons I Heart Umami Sesame Chicken Sauce (page 186)

White sesame seeds

Chopped scallions

Broccoli florets or a simple mixed green salad of your choice

MEAL-PLANNING

Make the sauce ahead of time and store in a glass container in the refrigerator. Thinly slice and marinate the chicken and store in the refrigerator if using the next day, or otherwise in the freezer. Defrost overnight in the refrigerator before cooking.

I absolutely adore this American take on the traditional Chinese dish. The chicken is juicy, tender, and coated with my homemade Sesame Chicken Sauce that's sweetened with dates (page 186). I highly recommend that you not miss this one of my signature dishes.

1. PREPARE THE CHICKEN: Chop the chicken into bite-sized pieces, place in a medium bowl, and add the remaining chicken ingredients, except the oil. Mix well and set aside.

2. Heat a large stainless-steel skillet over low heat until well heated, 4 to 5 minutes, then add 2 tablespoons avocado oil and panfry the chicken in several batches (do not overcrowd the skillet). Don't touch or move the chicken pieces until you see the bottom layer is golden brown, about 3 minutes. Flip the chicken and cook until the chicken is 90 to 95 percent cooked through, about 2 minutes. Remove the chicken and its juices from the skillet and set aside.

3. START THE STIR-FRY: Add a bit more avocado oil to the skillet used for the chicken and sauté the ginger and garlic, along with a sprinkle of salt, until fragrant. Add 3 to 4 heaping tablespoons of the sesame chicken sauce, stir-fry the aromatics with the sauce for 8 to 10 seconds, then add the chicken back to the skillet. Coat the chicken with the sauce and stir-fry for a few more minutes, until completely cooked through.

4. Serve hot and immediately, garnished with sesame seeds and chopped scallions, and accompanied by steamed broccoli florets or any simple mixed green salad.

VELVET CASHEW CHICKEN STIR-FRY

ACTIVE TIME: 30 TO 35 MINUTES | SERVES 4

CHICKEN:

1½ pounds chicken breasts, very thinly sliced (think: sashimi)

1 large egg white, beaten lightly

½ teaspoon sea salt

Pinch of ground white pepper

¾ tablespoon arrowroot starch

STIR-FRY SAUCE:

2 tablespoons coconut aminos

1 tablespoon fish sauce (Red Boat brand preferred)

¼ teaspoon arrowroot starch

STIR-FRY:

2½ to 3½ tablespoons avocado oil, plus more if needed

1 small yellow onion, diced

1 red bell pepper, diced

1 green bell pepper, diced, or ¾ pint shishito peppers, diced

3 garlic cloves, minced

Coarse salt

Ground white pepper

3 teaspoons finely chopped fresh ginger

2 tablespoons harissa chili paste (Entube brand preferred) or, for a nonspicy version, tomato paste

⅓ cup raw cashews

The word velvet *sounds fancy, but in fact it's a super simple technique that anyone can master at home. You'll never eat a bowl of dry chicken breasts after learning this easy trick—my signature formula to make chicken tender. This dish is super addictive. You'll find yourself wanting more!*

1. MARINATE THE CHICKEN: Combine the sliced chicken in a medium bowl with the other chicken ingredients. Mix everything well. Set aside in the refrigerator.

2. VELVET THE CHICKEN: Bring a pot of water to a boil, then lower the temperature to a simmer. Add 1 tablespoon avocado oil, then add the marinated chicken. Stir the water gently to separate the chicken pieces and prevent them from sticking to one another. After about 1 minute, or as soon as the chicken turns white, remove the chicken from the pot and drain well. (Note: The chicken is not cooked through at this stage. It will finish cooking in step 6.) Set the chicken aside.

3. PREPARE THE STIR-FRY SAUCE: Combine all the sauce ingredients in a small bowl.

4. START THE STIR-FRY: In a large sauté pan, heat 1½ tablespoons of the avocado oil over high heat, then sauté the onion and bell peppers with a pinch of salt and white pepper. When the onion just turns translucent and the bell peppers are still crunchy, remove them from the pan and set aside in a large serving bowl along with any juices from the skillet.

5. Using the same sauté pan (there should be no liquid juices in the pan), heat the remaining 1 to 2 tablespoons of avocado oil over medium-high heat. When hot, add the garlic, ginger, harissa paste, and a small pinch of salt.

continued

Stir-fry for about 10 seconds, or until fragrant. If the mixture seems too dry when sautéing, add a bit more oil.

6. Drain the chicken well. Make sure there's no additional liquid before adding the meat to the garlic mixture in the skillet. Stir-fry for 1 minute, then add the stir-fry sauce. Keep stir-frying until the chicken is cooked through. A few minutes before turning off the heat, add the cashews to the sauté pan. Coat with the sauce (see note) and season with white pepper to taste.

7. To serve, pour the sauce, chicken, and cashews over the bell peppers and onions. Serve hot.

Note

If there's a lot of liquid in the sauté pan after the chicken pieces are cooked through, remove the chicken with a slotted spoon and reduce the sauce over high heat for 2 to 3 minutes, then pour the sauce over the chicken and bell peppers.

MEAL-PLANNING

Thinly slice the chicken and store in the refrigerator if using the next day, or otherwise in the freezer. Defrost overnight in the refrigerator before cooking. Prechop the bell peppers and onions. Pat dry and store them in produce-saver containers in the refrigerator. Prechopped vegetables are best used within 2 to 3 days for maximum crispness and freshness.

DUTCH OVEN WHOLE ROASTED RED CURRY CHICKEN

ACTIVE TIME: 25 MINUTES | BAKE TIME: 1 HOUR 10 MINUTES | SERVES 4

One 3½-pound whole chicken (remove any giblets inside)

About 7 heaping tablespoons I Heart Umami Curry Flavor Enhancer (page 184)

1½ tablespoons ghee

2 heaping tablespoons store-bought red curry paste (Thai Kitchen brand preferred)

One 14-ounce can full-fat coconut milk

One 5.4-ounce can coconut cream (optional, but will make the chicken even tastier)

1 cup chicken stock

1 tablespoon fish sauce (Red Boat brand preferred)

3 to 4 medium carrots, diced into large chunks

2 tablespoons coconut oil

1 medium Italian eggplant or 2 Chinese eggplants, diced into bite-sized pieces

2 to 3 medium zucchini, diced into bite-sized pieces

Salt

Lime zest

Chopped fresh Thai or Italian basil

This is the perfect comfort food. The chicken is braised in my signature Curry Flavor Enhancer (page 184). The result is juicy chicken in a creamy aromatic broth. It's perfect for advance preparation or for a weekend family meal. This is a wonderful celebratory dish you'll enjoy making over and over again.

1. Preheat the oven to 400°F.

2. Rub 3 heaping tablespoons of the curry flavor enhancer over the entire chicken.

3. Heat the ghee in a large (6-quart) Dutch oven over medium-high heat, then lower the heat to medium. Add 2 heaping tablespoons of the red curry paste and the remaining 4 heaping tablespoons of curry flavor enhancer. Sauté until fragrant, about 15 seconds.

4. Place the seasoned chicken, breast side down, in the Dutch oven. Slightly brown the surface of the chicken, then flip the bird to brown the other side (3 to 4 minutes total). (Note: Take care not to burn the bottom of the pot as you brown the chicken; if the Dutch oven becomes too hot, lower the heat.)

5. Add the coconut milk, coconut cream, chicken stock, and fish sauce to the pot. Give it a gentle stir and scrape up any pieces stuck to the bottom of the pot. Turn the chicken breast-side up.

6. Cover the Dutch oven with a lid and transfer to the oven. Roast the chicken for 40 minutes.

continued

7. Add the carrots. Spoon a few tablespoons of the broth over the chicken breast to keep it moist. Return the pot to the oven to roast, covered, for another 20 minutes.

8. Remove the lid and increase the oven temperature to 425°F. Roast for 10 more minutes, or until the internal temperature of the chicken reaches 165°F on a meat thermometer.

9. Meanwhile, during the last 20 minutes of baking, heat the coconut oil in a large sauté pan over medium-high heat. Add the eggplant and zucchini, and season with salt to taste. Sauté until the eggplant is blistered and the zucchini turns softer and sweet but still has some crunch. Remove from the heat and set aside.

10. When the chicken is completely cooked through, remove from the oven and add the sautéed eggplant and zucchini to the Dutch oven.

11. Serve garnished with the lime zest and chopped basil.

MEAL-PLANNING

Follow the instructions through step 10. Remove the bones and shred the chicken into bite-sized pieces. Let cool before storing in the refrigerator or freezer. Reheat over the stovetop and garnish with the lime zest and basil just before serving.

SAVORY TAIWANESE ROASTED CHICKEN THIGH STEAKS

ACTIVE TIME: 10 MINUTES | MARINATE TIME: 30 MINUTES OR OVERNIGHT
BAKE TIME: 20 MINUTES | SERVES 4

4 boneless chicken thighs, skin on (about 2 pounds)

Coarse sea salt and freshly ground black pepper

3 to 4 large garlic cloves, grated or crushed

1 tablespoon grated fresh ginger

1 tablespoon toasted sesame oil

3 tablespoons coconut aminos

Cooking spray or oil

Chopped fresh parsley or scallions

Lemon wedges

This is one of my favorite ways to enjoy roasted chicken thighs. The chicken is first marinated and then roasted until golden and delicious. I highly recommend that you leave the skin on the chicken thighs for the best flavor and texture. Ask the butcher to remove the thigh bones.

1. Season both sides of the chicken with the salt and pepper. Combine the garlic, ginger, toasted sesame oil, and coconut aminos in a small bowl. Pour the marinade over the chicken thighs and use your hands to massage the sauce in evenly. Marinate overnight or set aside in the refrigerator for at least 30 minutes.

2. Preheat the oven to 425°F. Line a sheet pan with parchment paper and place a baking rack on top. Lightly spray or brush oil over the rack.

3. Place the chicken thighs, skin side up, on the prepared rack and bake for 20 minutes, or until the skin is light golden brown and the meat is completely cooked through. Then, set the oven to HIGH BROIL and broil for 3 minutes to give the skin a nice golden color. If using skinless chicken, broil on HIGH BROIL for only 1 to 2 minutes.

4. Sprinkle with chopped parsley or scallions and serve immediately with lemon wedges.

MEAL-PLANNING

It's best to marinate the chicken overnight. Store in a glass container in the refrigerator if using the next day, or otherwise in the freezer. Defrost overnight in the refrigerator before baking.

JAPANESE SEA SALT AND LEMON BAKED CHICKEN

ACTIVE TIME: 20 MINUTES | BAKE TIME: 35 MINUTES | SERVES 4

2 teaspoons coarse sea salt

1 teaspoon freshly ground black pepper

½ teaspoon ground ginger

1 teaspoon garlic powder

4 large skin-on, bone-in chicken legs (2 to 2½ pounds)

6 tablespoons coconut aminos

Juice of 1 lemon

2 tablespoons ghee, avocado, or coconut oil

Lemon wedges for serving

This Japanese-inspired dish is absolutely delicious and ridiculously simple to prepare. It's also a fuss-free recipe that's perfect to make ahead. I highly recommend that you marinate the chicken legs overnight and when you are ready to eat, simply bake them in the oven until crispy, juicy, and yummy! Serve with your favorite fresh leafy green salad.

1. Combine the salt, pepper, ginger, and garlic in a small bowl.

2. Use a fork to pierce a few holes all over the chicken legs (both meaty and skin parts). Gently rub the chicken with the spice mixture, both over the skin and in between the skin and the meat. Combine the coconut aminos and lemon juice in an airtight glass container. Place the chicken legs meaty side down and skin side up so they can soak up more flavor and let marinate overnight.

3. The next day, preheat the oven to 400°F. Line a baking sheet with parchment paper and place a baking rack on top. Heat 2 tablespoons of the ghee in a large cast-iron skillet over medium-high heat, then lower the heat to medium. Slightly drip the marinade off the chicken and place the legs, skin side down, in the pan. Panfry that side until golden brown, 7 to 8 minutes. Flip the chicken and panfry for an additional 5 to 6 minutes.

4. Transfer the chicken to the prepared baking sheet. Pour the pan drippings over the legs and bake on the lower rack for 35 minutes, or until the thickest part of the legs reaches 165°F on a meat thermometer (check after 25 minutes).

5. Remove the pan from the oven and allow the chicken to rest for 5 to 10 minutes before slicing. Serve hot with lemon wedges and salad.

SUPER FLAVORFUL EASY CHICKEN CURRY

ACTIVE TIME: 35 TO 40 MINUTES | SERVES 5 TO 6

CHICKEN:

1½ pounds chicken breast (or shrimp)

2 tablespoons curry powder

1 teaspoon sea salt (omit if using shrimp)

1 teaspoon freshly ground black pepper (reduce to ¼ teaspoon if using shrimp)

1 tablespoon olive oil

CURRY:

2 tablespoons coconut oil or ghee

2 teaspoons red curry paste (Thai Kitchen brand preferred)

3½ tablespoons I Heart Umami Curry Flavor Enhancer (page 184)

One 14-ounce can full-fat coconut milk

Lime wedges for serving

Have you had a really good bowl of Thai chicken curry? My signature Curry Flavor Enhancer (page 184) will transcend any store-bought or restaurant takeout version and bring your curry to the next level. This dish is perfect for batch cooking in advance and you'll never make a pot of curry without this recipe! You can also make this curry with shrimp. Serve over my Simple Cauli Fried Rice (page 162), and with any leafy greens of your choice.

1. MARINATE THE CHICKEN: Slice the chicken into pieces ⅛ inch thick and place in a bowl. Coat with the remaining chicken ingredients and let marinate for 15 to 20 minutes in the refrigerator.

2. START THE CURRY: Heat the coconut oil in a wok or sauté pan over medium-high heat, then lower the heat to medium. Add the red curry paste and curry flavor enhancer and stir-fry until fragrant, 10 to 15 seconds. Add the coconut milk. Lower the heat to medium-low. Cover with a lid and let simmer until slightly thickened, about 4 to 5 minutes.

3. Add the chicken and cook over medium heat until the meat is cooked through, 8 to 10 minutes. If using shrimp, simmer gently until the shrimp curl up and turn pink. Serve with lime wedges.

MEAL-PLANNING

Complete all the cooking steps. Let cool before storing in the refrigerator or freezer. The curry tastes even better the day after. If the sauce becomes too thick, thin it with a bit of chicken stock or more coconut milk. Reheat over the stovetop.

COCONUT MILK MEATBALLS

ACTIVE TIME: 15 TO 20 MINUTES | BAKE TIME: 35 MINUTES
SERVES 4 TO 5 (MAKES ABOUT 20 MEATBALLS)

MEATBALLS:

¾ cup fresh cilantro

2 small shallots

¾ cup diced carrot

¼ cup fresh basil leaves

1½ teaspoons grated fresh ginger

1 tablespoon fish sauce (Red Boat brand preferred)

½ teaspoon salt

½ teaspoon ground cumin

2 tablespoons coconut cream

2 pounds ground meat, such as pork, chicken (50% breast, 50% thigh), turkey, lamb, or veal

SAUCE:

One 14-ounce can full-fat coconut milk

1 tablespoon red curry paste (Thai Kitchen brand preferred)

1 teaspoon fish sauce (Red Boat brand preferred)

1 tablespoon no-sugar-added tomato paste

¼ teaspoon ground coriander

¼ teaspoon garam masala

TO SERVE:

Fresh lime juice

Cilantro

These meatballs are influenced by Thai and Southeast Asian curries. The recipe is extremely flexible. You can use any type of ground meat you have handy. We like a combination of pork and chicken or all lamb. The meatballs are roasted in the oven (less mess) and coated with a luscious dairy-free cream sauce. They are absolutely out of this world.

1. Preheat the oven to 400°F. Line a large sheet pan with parchment paper.

2. PREPARE THE MEATBALLS: Place the cilantro, shallots, carrot, basil, and ginger in a food processor and process until finely chopped. Add the fish sauce, salt, cumin, and coconut cream and blend well.

3. Mix the ground meat with the processed seasoning mixture. Mix well and form golf ball–sized meatballs (about 20 meatballs). Place on the prepared pan. Bake for 20 minutes, then flip the meatballs and bake for 15 minutes, or until the meatballs are completely cooked through.

4. Meanwhile, combine the sauce ingredients in a large saucepan and simmer slowly, stirring, over medium-low heat, until everything is combined and thickened (similar to a tomato soup consistency). Taste to see whether more salt, tomato paste, or red curry paste is needed. Keep stirring the sauce to prevent it from burning on the bottom.

5. Once the meatballs are cooked through and the sauce is thickened, add the meatballs to the sauce. Simmer for another 3 minutes, coating the meatballs with the sauce.

6. Drizzle with lime juice and garnish with cilantro leaves before serving.

MEAL-PLANNING

Prepare the sauce and store in a glass container in the refrigerator for up to 1 week. Prepare the meatballs through step 3. Let cool and store the roasted meatballs in the refrigerator if using within 3 days, or otherwise in the freezer. To serve, reheat meatballs in the sauce. You might need to add more coconut milk to thin the sauce a bit.

MEAL-PLANNING

Prepare the recipe through step 4 and remove from the heat. Once the meat sauce has cooled to room temperature, transfer to airtight containers and top with the broccoli, tomato, and cauliflower rice, if using. Seal and store in the refrigerator for up to 4 days. Reheat on the stovetop or in a microwave.

CHINESE MEAT SAUCE WITH EGGPLANT

ACTIVE TIME: 35 TO 40 MINUTES | SERVES 4

2½ tablespoons ghee

2 large garlic cloves, minced

1 large shallot, minced

1½ tablespoons finely chopped fresh ginger

3 scallions, chopped and separated into white and green parts

½ teaspoon red pepper flakes (optional)

Salt

½ pound ground pork

½ pound ground chicken or turkey

1 teaspoon toasted sesame oil

1½ teaspoons tomato paste

2 to 3 Italian eggplants, cut into large bite-sized cubes

Optional toppings: broccoli florets, cherry tomatoes, cauliflower rice (as much as you like)

STIR-FRY SAUCE:

3 tablespoons coconut aminos

1 tablespoon toasted sesame oil

1½ tablespoons fish sauce (Red Boat brand preferred)

1½ tablespoons aged balsamic vinegar

½ cup chicken or vegetable stock

½ teaspoon freshly ground black pepper

1 teaspoon grated fresh ginger

This is a savory meat sauce with melt-in-your-mouth eggplant and tons of fresh aromatics! Serve over zucchini noodles, cauliflower rice, or mashed sweet potatoes. This is the perfect dish to prepare in advance of a busy week.

1. Melt 1 tablespoon of the ghee in a large sauté pan, then add the garlic, shallot, ginger, white scallion parts, and red pepper flakes, if using. Season with a small pinch of salt. Sauté until fragrant, about 10 seconds. Add the ground pork and chicken and use a wooden spoon to further break up the meat into finger-sized pieces. Season with the sesame oil, tomato paste, and another small pinch of salt. Break the ground meat into finer pieces and cook until no longer pink, 8 to 10 minutes.

2. Combine the stir-fry sauce ingredients in a bowl and add to the sauté pan. Lower the heat to medium-low to low heat. Cover with a lid. Allow the meat sauce to simmer for 5 to 6 minutes.

3. Meanwhile, heat the remaining 1½ tablespoons of ghee in a separate large sauté pan and add the eggplant. Cook until the eggplant becomes soft and withered but not mushy, 6 to 9 minutes.

4. Add the cooked eggplant to the meat sauce. Give a quick toss. Garnish with the green scallion parts.

5. Serve topped with cherry tomatoes, broccoli florets, and/or cauliflower rice, if desired.

LION'S HEAD MEATBALLS

ACTIVE TIME: 35 MINUTES | SERVES 4 (MAKES ABOUT 12 MEATBALLS)

MEATBALLS:

1½ pounds ground pork (80% lean, 20% fat)

4 scallions, chopped

1 tablespoon grated fresh ginger

1½ tablespoons toasted sesame oil

2 tablespoons coconut aminos

½ teaspoon coarse sea salt

1 large shallot, chopped

1 large egg

2 teaspoons arrowroot starch, plus more for dusting

1½ tablespoons avocado oil

BRAISING MIX:

2 tablespoons avocado oil

3 thin slices fresh ginger

1 to 2 scallions

Coarse sea salt

¼ Napa or savoy cabbage, cut into 1- to 1½-inch-wide slices

1 cup chicken stock

2 tablespoons coconut aminos

2 teaspoons toasted sesame oil

2 to 3 baby bok choy, halved lengthwise (optional)

These Chinese meatballs get their name from their large size. They are soft, tender, and juicy, simmered in sweet and savory broth with savoy or Napa cabbage. They are my ultimate comfort food. These meatballs will keep your tummy happy.

1. PREPARE THE MEATBALLS: Place the pork and the remaining meatball ingredients, except the avocado oil, in a bowl. Gently mix and press the ground meat in a circular motion until the pork acquires a soft, pastelike texture. Form about 12 meatballs and lightly dust each meatball with a bit more arrowroot. Gently toss the meatballs from one hand to the other so that the arrowroot coheres well to the meatballs.

2. Heat the avocado oil in a large skillet over medium-high heat, then lower the heat to medium. Carefully sear the meatballs in batches until the surface is light golden brown but they are not cooked through. Remove from the heat and set aside.

3. PREPARE THE BRAISING MIX: In a wok, add the avocado oil and sauté the ginger and scallions over medium-high heat with a bit of salt until fragrant, about 10 seconds. Add the meatballs in a single layer. Add cabbage, placing the stems closer to the bottom of the wok and the leaves over the stems and meatballs. Add the chicken stock, coconut aminos, and sesame oil and season the cabbage with a little salt. Lower the heat to medium-low and cover with a lid. Cook until the meatballs are completely cooked through and the cabbage is tender, 20 to 25 minutes.

4. If using baby bok choy, add about 3 minutes before turning off the heat. Serve immediately, drizzling the meatballs with the broth.

MEAL-PLANNING

Proceed through step 2. Let the meatballs cool before storing in the refrigerator or freezer. If you wish, prewash and slice the cabbage, then pat dry and store in a produce saver in the refrigerator. Complete the recipe just before serving.

CHINESE PEPPER PORK LETTUCE CUPS

ACTIVE TIME: 20 TO 30 MINUTES | SERVES 4

PORK:

1 pound pork tenderloin or boneless loin roast

2 tablespoons coconut aminos

¼ teaspoon coarse sea salt

1 teaspoon toasted sesame oil

¼ teaspoon ground ginger

½ teaspoon arrowroot starch

Freshly ground black pepper

STIR-FRY:

2 teaspoons toasted sesame oil

1½ tablespoons coconut aminos

2 teaspoons harissa chili paste (Entube brand preferred)

Cooking fat or oil of your choice

2 large garlic cloves, minced

3 to 4 thin slices fresh ginger, cut into thin strips

Coarse sea salt

Green chile peppers (such as Anaheim, jalapeño, or serrano) or 1 green bell pepper, seeded and sliced matchstick thin

TO SERVE:

Iceberg or romaine lettuce

I adore stir-fry dishes and this recipe reminds me of my mom's cooking. Choose which chile peppers you use based on personal preference, or even make a nonspicy version with green bell peppers if you have small kids at home.

1. PREPARE THE PORK: Slice the pork into very thin strips (if the weather is hot, chill the meat in the freezer for 10 minutes before slicing) and marinate in a bowl with the remaining pork ingredients.

2. START THE STIR-FRY: Combine 2 teaspoons sesame oil, 1½ tablespoons coconut aminos, and harissa in a small bowl. Set aside.

3. Heat 1 tablespoon of cooking fat in a large skillet or wok over medium-high heat, then lower the heat to medium. Stir-fry the pork until it is no longer pink and becomes golden brown. Remove the pork from the pan and set aside.

4. Add a bit more cooking fat to the skillet used for the pork, sauté the garlic and fresh ginger, and season with a little bit of coarse sea salt. You should smell a nice aroma within 10 seconds. Add the chile peppers and a little more salt. Keep stir-frying for another 5 to 10 seconds. Add the pork back to the skillet along with the sesame oil mixture. Toss everything to combine.

5. Serve immediately with lettuce wraps.

MEAL-PLANNING

Thinly slice and marinate the pork. Store in the refrigerator for next-day use or in the freezer for later use. Defrost in the refrigerator before cooking.

CHINESE PEPPER STEAK

ACTIVE TIME: 25 TO 30 MINUTES | SERVES 4

BEEF:

1 pound sirloin steak

2 tablespoons coconut aminos

¼ teaspoon garlic powder

¼ teaspoon onion powder

2 teaspoons toasted sesame oil

1 teaspoon arrowroot starch

Scant ½ teaspoon baking soda

Coarse salt and freshly ground black pepper

STIR-FRY:

Cooking fat or oil of your choice

3 to 4 garlic cloves, thinly sliced

1 large shallot, sliced into thin strips

Salt

1 green bell pepper, sliced into thin strips

1 red bell pepper, sliced into thin strips

¼ cup I Heart Umami Paleo Worcestershire Sauce (page 188)

Love a good order of Chinese takeout? Then, you certainly don't want to miss my healthy (and much tastier) version of this famous takeout recipe. Serve with cauliflower rice, mashed potatoes, or a simple salad. No chopping or cooking is required for the homemade Paleo Worcestershire Sauce (page 188). Just mix well and store in the refrigerator for up to two weeks.

1. Thinly slice the beef against the grain and place in a bowl. Add the remaining beef ingredients. Mix well and set aside in the refrigerator while you prep the stir-fry ingredients.

2. START THE STIR-FRY: In a well-heated large, stainless-steel skillet, heat 1½ tablespoons of cooking fat and pan-sear the beef in batches until slightly charred. Remove the beef and any juices from the skillet and set aside.

3. Add a bit more cooking fat to the skillet used for the beef and add the garlic and shallot. Season with a little salt and sauté until fragrant, 8 to 10 seconds. Add the bell peppers and season with a bit more salt. Sauté until the peppers become slightly softer yet are still crunchy. Add the Worcestershire sauce, then add the beef back to the skillet. Give a quick toss to coat the meat with the sauce. Taste to see whether more salt or sauce is preferred.

4. Serve hot and immediately.

MEAL-PLANNING

Make the Worcestershire sauce and store in a glass container in the refrigerator for up to 2 weeks. Thinly slice and marinate the beef, and store in a separate glass container in the refrigerator if using the next day, or in the freezer for later use. Defrost in the refrigerator before cooking.

ASIAN BEEF MEATBALLS

ACTIVE TIME: 15 TO 20 MINUTES | BAKE TIME: 25 MINUTES
SERVES 4 (MAKES ABOUT 18 MEATBALLS)

MEATBALLS:

Coconut oil

1½ pounds ground beef

1½ teaspoons coarse sea salt

2 tablespoons coconut aminos

2 tablespoons toasted sesame oil

1½ tablespoons sweet potato flour or arrowroot starch

1 cup finely chopped carrot

½ small yellow onion, diced

1 cup flat-leaf parsley, finely chopped

3 scallions, finely chopped

1½ tablespoons grated fresh ginger

VEGETABLE NOODLES (OPTIONAL):

1½ teaspoons cooking fat of your choice

1 teaspoon minced garlic

Butternut squash, sweet potato, or turnip spiralized noodles

Salt and freshly ground black pepper

Juicy and umami-packed, these meatballs are baked in a muffin tin to preserve the juices, which you can use as dressing over squash noodles. Perfectly delicious!

1. Preheat the oven to 400°F. Lightly grease 18 muffin tin wells with the coconut oil.

2. PREPARE THE MEATBALLS: Combine the ground beef and remaining meatball ingredients in a bowl. Mix well. Form 18 meatballs, using your hands to gently apply some pressure to the meat mixture to make sure the chopped veggies and ground meat cohere well.

3. Place the meatballs in the prepared muffin tin. Bake for about 15 minutes, then use a small spoon to carefully flip the meatballs. Bake the flip side for an additional 10 minutes.

4. MEANWHILE, PREPARE THE VEGETABLE NOODLES, IF USING: Heat the cooking fat in a large skillet over medium-high heat, then lower the heat to medium and add the garlic and vegetable noodles. Give them a quick stir-fry until the noodles are softened yet still crisp. Season with salt and pepper to taste.

5. To serve, place the meatballs over the vegetable noodles. Scoop out the meatball juices from inside the muffin tin and use as dressing over the meatballs and noodles.

MEAL-PLANNING

After baking, let the meatballs cool, then pack them into glass containers and store in the refrigerator. Try not to overcrowd them. Pour the juices that remain in the muffin tin into a separate container or jar. Consume within 1 week, reheating the meatballs and their juices on the stovetop in a medium saucepan and sautéing the vegetable noodles, if using, right before serving.

CRISPY SESAME BEEF

ACTIVE TIME: 25 TO 35 MINUTES | SERVES 3 TO 4

1 pound sirloin steak

¼ cup arrowroot starch, plus 2 tablespoons for sautéing

½ teaspoon coarse sea salt

Freshly ground black pepper

¼ teaspoon garlic granules

¼ teaspoon onion granules

2 tablespoons ghee

⅓ cup I Heart Umami Sesame Beef Sauce (page 187)

Suggested toppings/add-ons: blanched green beans, carrot slices, sugar snap peas, broccoli florets

Toasted white sesame seeds

Thinly sliced sirloin steak is panfried to a golden crisp and coated with a sweet and tart sauce. Pair with light and refreshing vegetables for a deeply satisfying meal that won't weigh you down!

1. The sirloin steak against the grain into thin strips. Place in a bowl and toss to coat with ¼ cup of the arrowroot, the sea salt, black pepper, garlic granules, and onion granules. Cover and store in the refrigerator while preparing the sauce.

2. Heat the ghee in a large skillet over medium-high heat, then lower the heat to medium. Meanwhile, toss the marinated beef strips with the remaining 2 tablespoons of arrowroot, coating well and evenly. Test the heat with one beef strip first to see whether it starts to sizzle right away. Panfry the rest of the strips in batches, trying not to overcrowd the skillet and adding more ghee if necessary. Don't worry if some strips stick to each other.

3. When the beef strips are golden brown and crispy, add the sauce. Gently toss to combine. Serve immediately with blanched vegetables and garnish with sesame seeds.

MEAL-PLANNING

Make the sauce and store it in a glass container in the refrigerator for up to 2 weeks. Thinly slice and season the beef, then store in a glass container in the refrigerator if using the next day, or in the freezer for later use. Defrost in the refrigerator before cooking.

ELECTRIC PRESSURE COOKER VIETNAMESE BEEF STEW

ACTIVE TIME: 15 MINUTES | PRESSURE COOKER TIME: 30 MINUTES | SERVES 5 TO 6

BEEF:

2 pounds beef short ribs or chuck shoulder

1 to 1½ tablespoons grated fresh ginger

1 to 2 teaspoons chili powder (optional)

1 teaspoon ground cinnamon (I used Vietnamese cinnamon)

2 teaspoons curry powder

2 tablespoons fish sauce (Red Boat brand preferred)

1½ teaspoons sea salt

¼ teaspoon freshly ground black pepper

2 tablespoons olive oil

SOUP:

2 tablespoons coconut or avocado oil

1 large onion, diced

6 garlic cloves, sliced

2 lemongrass stalks, tough outer layers removed, chopped, or zest of ½ lemon

1½ teaspoons coarse salt

2 to 3 large carrots, diced into large chunks (for an electric pressure cooker) or bite-sized pieces (for stovetop)

This Vietnamese-inspired dish also reminds me of Chinese beef stew very much because of the use of star anise and cinnamon. Traditionally lemongrass is used in Vietnamese beef stew; you can replace it with lemon zest if lemongrass is not available. Star anise pods add a wonderful fragrance. You can replace the pods with powdered star anise, if necessary.

1. MARINATE THE BEEF: Cut the beef into 1¼- to 1½-inch cubes. Place in a bowl with the remaining beef ingredients, using your hands to coat well. Set aside in the refrigerator while preparing the vegetables.

2. MAKE THE SOUP: Select the SAUTÉ function on the electric pressure cooker and place the coconut oil in the pot (see page 110 for stove-top instructions). When hot, add the onion, garlic, and lemongrass. Season with a bit of salt and sauté until fragrant. Add the marinated beef cubes. Sear the cubes on all sides and season with a pinch of salt. Add the carrots and daikon radish. Sauté for a few more minutes, then turn off the electric pressure cooker. Add the cup of beef stock and the tomato paste and star anise pods. Give a stir to ensure nothing is stuck to the bottom of the pot. Close the lid, seal the valve, press MANUAL, and select HIGH PRESSURE for 30 minutes.

3. Meanwhile, preheat the oven to 425°F. Line a large baking sheet with parchment paper.

continued

2 cups daikon radish, peeled and diced into larger chunks (for an electric pressure cooker), or bite-sized pieces (for stovetop) (optional)

1 cup beef stock (for an electric pressure cooker), or 2 cups (for stovetop)

¼ cup tomato paste

2 star anise pods, or 1 teaspoon powder

2 medium yams or sweet potatoes, diced into bite-sized pieces (use as much as you'd like)

Olive oil

2 to 3 teaspoons arrowroot starch (optional)

1 large bunch curly kale (use as much as you'd like), chopped

4. Lightly season the diced yams with salt and olive oil and place on the prepared baking sheet. Bake for 20 minutes, lower the heat to 400°F, flip, and bake the yams for 10 more minutes, or until the yams are soft, tender, and golden brown.

5. When the electric pressure cooker finishes cooking, use natural release for 5 minutes, then manual quick release. Test whether the beef is tender to your liking. If not, add 10 more minutes to the cooking time.

6. If there is too much liquid, scoop out the beef cubes, carrots, and daikon and turn on the SAUTÉ function. In a small bowl, mix 2 to 3 teaspoons of arrowroot starch with 1 to 2 tablespoons of cold water to make a slurry. Add the slurry to the boiling broth and gently stir the broth until thickened, about 1 minute. Add the beef and veggies back to the pot. Stir in the chopped kale. Taste to see whether more salt or fish sauce is needed.

7. To serve, ladle the beef cubes, stewed vegetables, and roasted yams in a serving bowl. Drizzle with a few tablespoons of the pot liquid. Serve hot and immediately.

STOVETOP COOKING:

After step 1, heat the coconut oil in a Dutch oven or heavy-bottomed large soup pot over medium-high heat, then add the onion, garlic, and lemongrass. Season with a bit of salt and sauté until fragrant. Add the marinated beef cubes. Sear the cubes on all sides and season with a pinch of salt. Add the 2 cups of beef stock and the tomato paste and star anise pods. Lower the heat to low and cook, covered, for about an hour, or until the beef is tender. (You might need to add extra stock during the cooking process, until the beef is fully cooked). Once the beef is tender, add the carrots and daikon. Cook for an additional 20 minutes, or until the vegetables are tender to your liking. Stir in the kale. If there is too much liquid, follow step 6, above, to thicken the sauce.

MEAL-PLANNING

If serving right away, you can skim the fat off the top of the stew, if preferred. Alternatively, store the stew in the refrigerator for up to 4 days, or in the freezer for 1 month! Reheat on the stovetop over medium heat.

JAPANESE HAMBURGER STEAK

ACTIVE TIME: 40 MINUTES | SERVES 6

Ghee

1 small onion, minced

Salt and freshly ground black pepper

⅔ pound ground beef

⅔ pound ground pork

1 large egg

½ cup almond flour, plus more if needed

¼ cup full-fat coconut milk

½ teaspoon ground nutmeg

1 tablespoon ghee or cooking fat of your choice

4 portobello mushrooms caps (optional) plus olive oil for brushing

⅔ cup I Heart Umami Paleo Worcestershire Sauce (page 188)

Cucumber slices (optional)

Small red radish slices (optional)

This Japanese take on hamburger patties is melt-in-your-mouth juicy and delicious. I pair them with a simple homemade Worcestershire sauce to give the burgers a nice tangy taste. This is the perfect dish for batch cooking in advance. When you are ready to eat, after defrosting and a quick grill, dinner will be ready in no time.

1. Heat a little ghee in a skillet over medium heat and sauté the onion until golden and soft. Season with a small pinch of salt and black pepper.

2. Combine the beef and pork, sautéed onion, egg, almond flour, coconut milk, and nutmeg in a large bowl. Season with salt and pepper. Mix everything well with your hands.

3. Take a golf ball–sized portion and form into a patty, then throw it from the palm of one hand to the other several times. This will enhance the texture of the patty and help hold its shape during cooking. If the mixture is too wet to form patties, return the first patty to the bowl and let the mixture chill in the refrigerator for 5 to 10 minutes. If it's still too wet, add a bit more almond flour.

4. Form the rest of the patties (you should have a total of 6 patties). Gently press the center of each patty with your finger to leave an indentation.

5. Heat 1 tablespoon of ghee in a large skillet over medium-high heat, then lower the heat to medium. Add the patties and sear the outside, 2 to 3 minutes per side.

6. Lower the heat to medium-low and continue to cook until the patties are completely cooked through. (You can cover with a lid, leaving a little opening for the steam to escape.

continued

This will ensure that the patties are cooked all the way through.) Transfer the patties to a plate and keep warm.

7. If using the portobello mushrooms: Brush the mushroom caps with olive oil. Season with salt and pepper. Grill over medium heat until the mushrooms soften.

8. Serve the patties immediately with Worcestershire sauce, the grilled mushrooms, and sliced cucumber and radish, if using.

MEAL-PLANNING

Make the Worcestershire sauce ahead of time. Form the burger patties and freeze them, uncooked, with parchment paper between each patty. Defrost overnight in the refrigerator before cooking.

CUMIN LAMB STIR-FRY

ACTIVE TIME: 40 MINUTES | SERVES 4

LAMB:

1 pound boneless lamb shoulder

3 teaspoons ground cumin

1½ teaspoons arrowroot starch

1½ tablespoons coconut aminos

¾ teaspoon chili powder (optional)

¾ teaspoon coarse salt, plus more for searing

1 tablespoon olive oil

Avocado or coconut oil, or cooking oil of your choice

AROMATICS:

3 scallions, sliced diagonally and separated into white and green parts

5 garlic cloves, sliced

1 large shallot, sliced into thin strips

2 teaspoons Sichuan peppercorns, ground

½ Fresno, serrano, or Thai chile, seeded and sliced into thin strips (optional)

Salt

Chopped fresh cilantro (as much or as little as you like; optional)

This recipe reminds me of my grandma who came to Taiwan from the northern part of China. Her dishes are always full of character and never shy away from using aromatics. This dish is bold on flavor and shows off its personality without relying on sauce. When in doubt, use more aromatics.

1. PREPARE THE LAMB: Thinly slice the lamb shoulder against the grain and mix well in a bowl with the remaining lamb ingredients, except the avocado oil.

2. Heat a large, dry, stainless-steel skillet over medium heat until well heated. When hot, add 2 tablespoons of avocado oil. Sear the lamb until slightly charred and almost cooked through. Season with a pinch of salt. Remove the lamb and juices from the skillet and set aside.

3. PREPARE THE AROMATICS: Reheat the skillet used for the lamb, adding a bit more avocado oil, and sauté the white scallion parts, garlic, shallot, ground Sichuan peppercorns, and chile. Season with salt and stir-fry briskly until fragrant, 10 to 15 seconds, taking care not to let the ingredients sit still and burn. Add the lamb back to the skillet. Toss everything to combine. Taste to see whether more salt is needed. Before turning off the heat, stir in the cilantro and green scallion parts. Serve hot and immediately.

MEAL-PLANNING

Thinly slice and marinate the lamb. Store in the refrigerator for next-day use, or in the freezer for later. Defrost in the refrigerator before cooking.

WEEK

BATCH COOK

WEEKEND

EASY

FLAVOR

NIGHT BFF

ING PERFECT

FUN

ADD-ONS

POP

Chinese Cabbage-Wrapped
Dim Sum (Shumai), page 124

Who says clean eating can't be fun? I love surprising my friends and family with these boldly flavored fresh meals at family gatherings. These Weekend Fun recipes are full of color, textural contrast, and flavor. They are complete meals that are high in healthy protein and fiber, and low in carbohydrates, which not only look gorgeous but are also very tasty. Kids and adults alike will have fun enjoying these dishes!

FILIPINO SKIRT STEAK AND CAULIFLOWER FRIED RICE BRUNCH

ACTIVE TIME: 20 MINUTES | MARINATE TIME: 1 TO 2 HOURS OR OVERNIGHT | SERVES 4

STEAK:

1 pound skirt steak

3 tablespoons coconut aminos

½ teaspoon coarse salt

Juice of ¼ lime

2 large garlic cloves, crushed

Freshly ground black pepper

1 tablespoon ghee

TOMATO TOPPING:

1 medium ripe tomato, finely chopped

1½ tablespoons finely chopped shallot

2 tablespoons finely chopped fresh
   flat-leaf parsley

Fresh lime juice

TO SERVE:

Simple Cauli Fried Rice (page 162)

4 large eggs, fried (optional)

Looking for a lovely brunch recipe for friends and family? This one will be sure to delight. Marinate the steak overnight for extra flavor. It's the perfect all-in-one healthy brunch!

1. MARINATE THE STEAK: Use a sharp knife to shallowly score the steak in small crisscross cuts to better enable marinating. Place the steak in a bowl with the remaining steak ingredients, except the ghee, and marinate overnight or for at least 1 to 2 hours in the refrigerator.

2. Melt the ghee in a well-heated cast-iron skillet. Shake the excess marinade off the steak and cook each side for 2 to 3 minutes for medium-rare, depending on the thickness of the cut, basting the steak with the ghee and steak juices. Set aside to rest.

3. In a small bowl, combine the tomato sauce ingredients, adding lime juice to taste.

4. To serve, slice the steak against the grain. Serve with the cauli rice and fried eggs, if using, and the tomato topping.

PALEO BUDDHA BOWLS WITH CRISPY VEGGIE PATTIES

ACTIVE TIME: 30 MINUTES | SERVES 4

PATTIES:

2 cups finely shredded or grated zucchini (see notes)

2 cups finely shredded or grated carrot

½ teaspoon coarse sea salt

⅔ cup cassava or almond flour

3 large eggs

3 tablespoons full-fat coconut milk

1 cup chopped scallions (or more if you'd like)

Freshly ground black pepper

Coconut or avocado oil, or ghee

SESAME TAHINI DRESSING:

3 tablespoons tahini

1½ tablespoons coconut aminos

½ teaspoon balsamic vinegar

½ teaspoon rice vinegar

1 teaspoon grated garlic

SUGGESTED ADD-ON ITEMS FOR BUDDHA BOWLS:

Green beans (blanched and shocked; see notes)

Sugar snap peas (blanched and shocked)

Broccoli florets (blanched and shocked)

Grape tomatoes

Zucchini ribbons

Radishes

These vegetable-packed patties are panfried to a golden brown crisp. They are gluten- and dairy-free. Feel free to change my suggested add-on items to make your own healthy Buddha bowls.

1. PREPARE THE PATTIES: Sprinkle the zucchini and carrot lightly with salt and set aside for 10 minutes.

2. Use a cheesecloth to squeeze out as much liquid from the salted vegetables as possible. Place the zucchini, carrot, and remaining patty ingredients, except the coconut oil, in a large bowl. Use a wooden spoon or your hands to gently mix well.

3. Line a sheet pan or plate with parchment paper. Scoop a little more than 2 tablespoons of filling and use your hands to shape into a small patty. Form 10 to 12 such patties and place them on the prepared pan.

4. Heat 1 tablespoon of coconut oil in a large sauté pan over medium-high heat, then lower the heat to medium. Panfry the patties in several batches until both sides are golden brown and cooked through, adding a bit more oil if needed. Transfer the patties to a large plate lined with paper towels.

5. Meanwhile, combine all the dressing ingredients in a small bowl along with 3 tablespoons water and mix well.

6. Serve with the veggies of your choice and the dressing on the side.

Notes

If you wish, you can use a food processor or chopper to chop the zucchini and carrot until really fine (as small as a grain of rice).

Blanch the green beans, snap peas, and broccoli quickly in boiling water, then shock them in cold water to stop the cooking and maintain a vibrant green color.

CHINESE CABBAGE-WRAPPED DIM SUM (SHUMAI)

ACTIVE TIME: 30 TO 35 MINUTES | STEAM TIME: 25 TO 30 MINUTES | SERVES 4

1 small cabbage, cored (see note)

1 pound ground pork

1½ tablespoons grated fresh ginger

1 large egg white, lightly beaten

1½ tablespoons toasted sesame oil

2 tablespoons coconut aminos

2 scallions, thinly sliced

6 tablespoons finely chopped carrot

1 teaspoon sea salt

½ teaspoon ground white pepper

¼ cup I Heart Umami Dim Sum Dumpling Dipping Sauce (page 188)

Simply by looking at the photo on page 118, you won't be able to tell that these low-carb shumai are wrapped in cabbage leaves. It takes a bit of time and patience to separate the leaves, so this dish is better for the weekend or special occasions. The result is juicy, savory meatballs wrapped in sweet cabbage and dipped in my signature Dim Sum Dumpling Dipping Sauce (page 188). Make extra because they will be gone in a hurry!

1. Fill a large pot with cold water just enough to cover the entire cabbage and bring the water to a boil. Add the whole cabbage, cored side down, and cook at a low boil for 10 to 15 minutes. Using tongs or chopsticks, gently remove the leaves as they separate. Set the leaves aside to cool. Be careful not to burn yourself with the boiling water.

2. To prepare the dumpling filling, combine the ground pork in a bowl with the remaining ingredients, except for the dipping sauce. Mix well.

3. Line a steamer with a thin layer of parchment paper, or place a heatproof plate over a steamer rack. Add only enough water to the pot to stay below the steamer.

4. Select a small cabbage leaf from the inner core of the cabbage. Holding the leaf in your hand, form a small cup shape and spoon about 1 tablespoon of the meat filling into the cupped leaf. Gently squeeze the cabbage leaf around the meat filling to make sure it adheres nicely. Repeat with the remaining leaves and filling.

Note

To remove the cabbage core, cut a deep, cone-shaped incision into the bottom of the cabbage. Alternatively, use a cabbage corer.

5. Place the dumplings in the prepared steamer, setting them close to each other so they won't fall apart in the steamer. Steam over high heat for 25 to 30 minutes, or until fully cooked. The water should be more than simmering but not quite boiling.

6. Before serving, combine the dipping sauce ingredients in a bowl. Serve the sauce on the side with the Paleo shumai!

SALTY CRUNCHY TAIWANESE CHICKEN NUGGETS

ACTIVE TIME: 40 TO 50 MINUTES | MARINATE TIME: 2 HOURS OR OVERNIGHT | SERVES 5

1½ pounds skinless chicken breasts or thighs

1½ teaspoons grated fresh ginger

2 large garlic cloves, grated

2 tablespoons coconut aminos

½ teaspoon Chinese five-spice powder

1 teaspoon fine sea salt

½ teaspoon ground white pepper

⅓ cup coconut oil, avocado oil, or ghee

1 cup fresh Thai or Italian basil leaves and stems

1 cup sweet potato flour or arrowroot starch

After growing up in Taiwan, this is the dish that I miss the most: chicken nuggets panfried to a golden brown crisp with a hint of basil. These mini nuggets are full of flavor and traditionally served without a dipping sauce. They make the perfect savory appetizer, game-day snack, or savory treat whenever you love some salty, crunchy yum!

1. Slice the chicken into bite-sized pieces. Place in a lidded container with the ginger, garlic, coconut aminos, five-spice powder, salt, and pepper. Gently stir and coat each piece of chicken with the marinade. Seal the container and refrigerate overnight or for at least 2 hours.

2. Heat the coconut oil in a deep skillet or Dutch oven. In the meantime, use a paper towel to pat the basil leaves dry. Lower the heat to medium-low, then carefully add the basil leaves, using a splatter guard to prevent the oil from splattering. Once the basil is crispy, about 5 seconds, remove from the pot and drain on paper towels.

3. Drain the chicken and discard the marinade. Toss and coat the chicken with sweet potato flour in a large resealable plastic bag. Heat the now basil-flavored oil over medium-high heat, then lower the heat to medium. Test the oil temperature with one piece of chicken: it should start bubbling right away. Add and panfry the chicken in several batches until completely cooked through and golden brown. Remove the chicken from the skillet and drain on paper towels. Add more oil if needed.

4. Place the crunchy chicken nuggets in a large bowl. Crush the fried basil over the chicken and, if you like, toss with more fine sea salt and white pepper. Serve immediately with salt and white pepper on the side for an authentic taste or with your favorite dipping sauce.

CRISPY CHICKEN WINGS WITH MALAYSIAN SWEET CHILI DIPPING SAUCE

ACTIVE TIME: 15 MINUTES | MARINATE TIME: OVERNIGHT | BAKE TIME: 40 MINUTES | SERVES 3

6 garlic cloves

1 thumb-sized piece fresh ginger

1 red Fresno or serrano chili, seeded

1 large shallot

½ pear, or 2 tablespoons applesauce

¼ cup coconut aminos

1 tablespoon fish sauce (Red Boat brand preferred)

Juice of ½ lime

1½ pounds chicken wings

I Heart Umami Malaysian-Inspired Chili Dipping Sauce (page 191)

White sesame seeds (optional)

These wings are savory and tangy, with a hint of spicy flavor. The trick is to marinate the wings overnight to deepen the flavor. Be sure to brush them with the chili dipping sauce for a lovely golden brown color!

1. Place the garlic, ginger, chile, shallot, and pear in a food processor or blender and blend until smooth. Add the coconut aminos, fish sauce, and lime juice and pulse a few more times until smooth. Place the chicken wings in a large bowl. Pour the marinade over the wings and turn them to coat them evenly. Store in the refrigerator overnight to absorb the flavor.

2. Preheat the oven to 425°F and place a wire rack over a sheet pan lined with parchment paper.

3. Drain the chicken and discard the marinade. Place the wings on the prepared pan. Bake for 20 minutes, then carefully flip the wings and bake for another 20 minutes.

4. Remove the wings from the oven. Lightly brush them with the dipping sauce. Send them back to the oven at HIGH BROIL for an additional 1 to 2 minutes Watch like a hawk to prevent them from burning.

5. Sprinkle with sesame seeds, if desired. Serve hot and immediately with the remaining dipping sauce.

Note

To use wakame, rehydrate a small handful of the dried seaweed in a bowl of cold water for 5 to 10 minutes, or until it has become completely rehydrated. Drain and use your hands to gently squeeze out any excess water. Set aside.

COLD RAMEN NOODLES

ACTIVE TIME: 30 TO 35 MINUTES | SERVES 3

1 large zucchini

2 to 3 skinless, boneless chicken thighs

Salt and freshly ground black pepper

Garlic powder

Onion powder

OTHER TOPPINGS (OPTIONAL AND AS MUCH AS YOU LIKE):

Spinach

6 to 10 shrimp, peeled and deveined

2 or 3 large eggs

Sliced radish

Japanese wakame seaweed (see note)

Chopped scallions

COLD RAMEN DRESSING:

3 tablespoons coconut aminos

1½ tablespoons rice vinegar

1 tablespoon toasted sesame oil

¾ to 1 teaspoon grated fresh ginger

Several drops hot sesame oil (optional)

Love a chilled bowl of Japanese ramen noodles? This low-carb ramen "noodle" bowl hits all the flavors and will not weigh you down. I added grilled chicken, shrimp, and vegetable toppings, but feel free to swap in anything you like.

1. Spiralize the zucchini to make zoodles. Cover and set aside in the refrigerator.

2. Lightly season both sides of the chicken thighs with salt, pepper, and garlic and onion granules. Grill the chicken thighs until they are completely cooked through. Set aside to cool, then slice.

3. PREPARE THE TOPPINGS: Bring a medium pot of water to a boil. Quickly blanch the spinach for a few seconds, then drain in a colander, rinse under cold running water, and let drip dry or gently squeeze out any excess water. Set aside. Use the same pot of boiling water to quickly blanch the shrimp until they just start to turn pink, about 20 to 30 seconds. Rinse under cold running water and set aside.

4. Soft boil the eggs, if using: Bring a second medium pot of water to a boil, lower the heat to a simmer, and carefully set the eggs in the boiling water. Cook for 7 minutes, gently pushing the eggs around in the pot to ensure even cooking on all sides. Remove the eggs from the pot and place them in an ice bath of water until they are cool to the touch. Gently tap the eggs and peel under cold running water. Slice in half right before serving.

5. MAKE THE DRESSING: Combine all the dressing ingredients in a small bowl along with 2 tablespoons cold water and mix well.

6. To assemble: Combine the zoodles, sliced grilled chicken, shrimp, spinach, eggs, and the rest of the topping ingredients in a medium serving bowl. Pour the dressing over all before serving.

CHICKEN YAKISOBA

ACTIVE TIME: 40 TO 45 MINUTES | SERVES: 5 TO 6 PEOPLE

YAKISOBA SWEET POTATO NOODLES:

1 white sweet potato (select a fat one)

2 tablespoons olive oil

Sprinkle of onion powder

Sprinkle of garlic powder

Coarse salt

CHICKEN:

1½ pounds skinless, boneless chicken thighs, sliced

½ teaspoon coarse salt

⅛ teaspoon freshly ground black pepper

⅛ teaspoon ground ginger

1½ teaspoons toasted sesame oil

¼ cup ghee or avocado oil

STIR-FRY:

3 scallions, chopped and separated into white and green parts

½ yellow onion, thinly sliced

3 garlic cloves, sliced

Salt

2 large carrots, cut into matchsticks

2 cups snow peas, roughly chopped on the diagonal

½ to 1 Napa, savoy, or green cabbage (4 cups sliced)

8 ounces fresh shiitake mushrooms, sliced

3 to 4 tablespoons I Heart Umami Paleo Worcestershire Sauce (page 188)

This Japanese-inspired dish is prepared with baked crispy, curly sweet potato noodles and a saucy chicken cabbage stir-fry. This two-in-one recipe is perfect for weekend entertainment. One bite and you'll be hooked for more!

White sweet potatoes give the noodles a crispier texture. For a lower-carb version, replace the sweet potato noodles with raw or lightly sautéed zucchini noodles or kelp or shirataki noodles, prepared according to the package directions.

1. Preheat the oven to 400°F. Line a large baking sheet with parchment paper.

2. Spiralize the sweet potato and season with the olive oil, onion and garlic powder, and salt. Arrange in a single layer on the prepared sheet pan and bake for 25 minutes. Remove from the oven and set aside to cool.

3. PREPARE THE CHICKEN: Season the sliced chicken thighs with salt, pepper, ginger, and sesame oil. Mix well and set aside.

4. Heat the ghee in a large skillet over medium-high heat and panfry the chicken slices until the edges are golden and almost cooked through. Remove the chicken and juices from the skillet and set aside.

5. Add the scallion white parts, sliced onion and garlic, and a little salt to the skillet used for the chicken and sauté until fragrant. Add the remaining stir-fry veggies, season with a little more salt, and sauté for a few more minutes.

continued

6. Add the Worcestershire sauce and return the chicken to the skillet. Taste and adjust the seasonings. Toss to combine.

7. Layer the sweet potato noodles at the bottom of a large serving bowl or tray. Ladle the chicken and veggies on top. Sprinkle with the green scallion parts. Serve immediately.

MEAL-PLANNING

Make the Worcestershire sauce ahead of time. Store in an airtight glass container in the refrigerator for up to 3 weeks. Slice and season the chicken thighs. Store in the refrigerator for next day use, or in the freezer for longer. If you like, prepare vegetables in advance and store them in vegetable-saver containers in the refrigerator.

PALEO PAD THAI SQUASH NOODLE STIR-FRY

ACTIVE TIME: 30 TO 35 MINUTES | BAKE TIME: 30 MINUTES | SERVES 5 TO 6

1 small spaghetti squash (about 2½ pounds)

Salt

CHICKEN AND SHRIMP:

4 skinless, boneless chicken thighs or breasts

7 or 8 medium shrimps, peeled and deveined (optional)

Chicken seasonings: salt, ground white pepper, garlic powder, onion powder, and red chili powder (optional)

1½ tablespoons ghee

PALEO PAD THAI SAUCE:

1¾ tablespoons fish sauce (Red Boat brand preferred)

2½ tablespoons tamarind concentrate

¼ teaspoon ground white pepper

STIR-FRY:

1½ tablespoons ghee or cooking fat of your choice

2 large garlic cloves, finely chopped

2 large shallots, finely chopped

½ teaspoon red pepper flakes (optional)

3 to 4 scallions, chopped and separated into white and green parts

In the recipe, I share a simple way to make the longest (nonsoggy) spaghetti squash noodles. Paired with my no-sugar-added pad thai stir-fry sauce, these noodles will satisfy your craving for Thai food!

1. PREPARE THE NOODLES: Preheat the oven to 400°F. Set a wire rack over a rimmed baking sheet.

2. Slice the ends off the squash, then cut widthwise into halves or rings. Run a knife around the interior of each piece to remove the seeds. Place the squash on the prepared rack and sprinkle both sides with salt. Let sit for 15 to 20 minutes to allow the salt to draw moisture out. Wipe away any excess salt and moisture.

3. Bake the squash for 30 minutes, rotating halfway through for even baking. Remove from the oven and allow to cool to room temperature, then peel the skin away and separate the strands into long "noodles."

4. PREPARE THE CHICKEN AND SHRIMP, IF USING: Slice the chicken into ¼-inch-thick slices and lightly sprinkle with salt, white pepper, garlic and onion powder, and red chili powder, if using. Mix well.

5. Heat the ghee in a large sauté pan or cast-iron skillet over medium-high heat, then lower the heat to medium. Cook the chicken until completely cooked through and golden brown.

6. Add the shrimp after the chicken is cooked through. As soon as the shrimp turn light pink, turn off the heat and set the pan aside.

continued

Salt

1 cup julienned carrot (or more if you'd like)

1 cup bean sprouts (or more if you'd like)

1 cup snow peas, roughly chopped

1 lime, cut into wedges

Small handful of cashews, roughly chopped (optional)

7. MAKE THE SAUCE: Combine all of the the pad thai sauce ingredients along with 1 tablespoon water in a small bowl, mix well, and set aside.

8. TO STIR-FRY: Heat the ghee in a large sauté pan or wok over medium-high heat, then lower the heat to medium. Add the garlic, shallots, red pepper flakes, and white scallion parts. Season with a small pinch of salt and sauté until fragrant, about 10 seconds. Add the carrot, bean sprouts, and snow peas. Keep stir-frying for another 5 seconds. Add the cooked chicken and shrimp, if using, and pad thai sauce and stir-fry for about 10 seconds. Add the squash noodles. Toss the noodles a few times to let the sauce coat the noodles evenly.

9. Serve immediately with lime wedges, the green scallion parts, and chopped cashews, if you like.

PALEO PAD SEE EW

ACTIVE TIME: 35 TO 40 MINUTES | SERVES 4

CHICKEN:

1¼ pounds chicken breasts

2 tablespoons olive oil

2 large garlic cloves, grated

1 teaspoon grated fresh ginger

3 teaspoons fish sauce (Red Boat brand preferred)

¾ to 1 tablespoon arrowroot starch

⅛ to ¼ teaspoon red pepper flakes (optional)

STIR-FRY:

2 tablespoons coconut aminos

2 teaspoons fish sauce (Red Boat brand preferred)

Pinch of ground white pepper (optional)

6 tablespoons avocado or coconut oil

2 to 3 large eggs

2 large garlic cloves, minced

3 to 4 Chinese dried red chiles (optional)

Salt

¾ pound broccolini, sliced on the diagonal

1 large zucchini, sliced into wide noodles (use a mandoline or julienne slicer)

This low-carb, gluten-free version of pad see ew—*Thai stir-fried wide noodles—comes with golden crispy fried eggs and juicy chicken in a light sauce that's naturally sweet and savory. The use of zucchini noodles makes it so healthy and absolutely delicious!*

1. Marinate the chicken: Thinly slice the chicken breasts. Mix well in a bowl with the remaining chicken ingredients. Set aside for 15 to 20 minutes in the refrigerator.

2. TO STIR-FRY: Combine the coconut aminos, fish sauce, and white pepper in a small bowl and set aside.

3. Preheat a large skillet over medium-high heat, then add 2 tablespoons of oil. Fry the eggs sunny-side up. I like to keep the yolk soft and runny while the bottom side that touches the skillet is crispy and golden brown. Set aside.

4. Preheat the same skillet over medium-high heat. When hot, add 2 more tablespoons of the oil. Panfry the chicken in one layer (do this in batches) until golden brown. Remove from the skillet and set aside.

5. Add the remaining 2 tablespoons of oil to the skillet and add the garlic and whole dried chiles. Season with little salt and sauté until fragrant. Add the broccolini. Keep sautéing for about 1 minute and season with more salt. Add the cooked chicken back to the pan. Add the fried eggs, breaking them into smaller pieces with a spatula as they cook. Add the zucchini noodles. Keep stir-frying until the noodles become more bendable, about 1 minute. Add the coconut aminos mixture. Give a quick toss and serve immediately.

ROMANTIC STEAMED SEAFOOD DIM SUM

ACTIVE TIME: 25 TO 30 MINUTES | SERVES 2

¾ pound skinless, boneless sea bass or other meaty fish fillets, cut into 2½-inch pieces

6 clams, scrubbed

6 shrimp

1 to 2 fresh full cap shiitake mushrooms

1 large carrot, sliced into coins

5 to 6 asparagus spears, trimmed (woody bottoms discarded)

3 tablespoons coconut aminos

1 tablespoon toasted sesame oil

Coarse salt and freshly ground black pepper

Lemon wedges (optional)

⅓ cup I Heart Umami Scallion-Ginger Dipping Oil (page 190)

Whenever we make dim sum at home, it reminds me of scenes in the Hong Kong-ese movies that show steamed seafood made in bamboo baskets. I simplify the traditional methods to make it easy to enjoy these dim sum in the comfort of your home. This recipe is low in carbs and packed with lean protein. The seafood is naturally sweet and savory and is delicious on its own without any dipping sauce, but if you like, try my Scallion-Ginger Dipping Oil (page 190) for an extra boost of flavor!

This dish is super versatile. When selecting fish, I recommend using white (meaty) fish fillets, such as sea bass, halibut, or cod, but you can substitute other seafood that you prefer. You can adjust the quantity of each ingredient based on your personal preference and the size of your steamer basket.

1. Place the fish, clams, shrimp, shiitake, and vegetables in a steamer basket lined with parchment paper or in a shallow, heatproof bowl so as to catch the juices. Season with the coconut aminos and sesame oil, and salt and pepper to taste.

2. Steam over medium to medium-low heat for 10 to 15 minutes. Remove from the pot and set aside the shrimp and asparagus. Steam the rest of the ingredients further until the fish is buttery and flaky and the clams are open.

3. Place the steamed ingredients in a serving bowl, straining the seafood juices through a sieve (save this stock for later use). Serve hot and immediately with lemon wedges, if using, and the dipping oil.

SWEET AND TART THAI-INSPIRED CRISPY TURMERIC FISH NUGGETS

ACTIVE TIME: 25 MINUTES | MARINATE TIME: 1 HOUR (BEST OVERNIGHT) | SERVES 3

FISH:

1¼ pounds fresh skinless, boneless cod fillet, cut into 2-inch pieces about ½ inch thick

1 tablespoon ground turmeric

1 teaspoon coarse salt, plus more for panfrying

2 teaspoons grated fresh ginger

2 tablespoons olive oil

2 teaspoons arrowroot starch

Coconut or avocado oil

MANGO SAUCE:

1 medium ripe mango

2 tablespoons rice vinegar

Juice of ½ lime

1 garlic clove, grated

1 teaspoon chili powder (optional)

SCALLION-DILL OIL:

2 tablespoons coconut or avocado oil

2 cups sliced scallion (cut into long, thin strips)

2 cups fresh dill

Sea salt

TOPPINGS:

Fresh cilantro (as much as you'd like)

Lime wedges

Chopped pine nuts, cashews, or almonds (optional)

This is a wonderful way to bring new flavor to crispy fish nuggets. The fish is panfried to a golden brown crisp and fragrant with fresh dill and scallion oil. Pair with sweet and tart mango lime dipping sauce for a refreshing dish!

1. Prepare the fish: Combine the cod in a bowl with the other fish ingredients, except the oil, and marinate for at least 1 hour in the refrigerator (best overnight).

2. Place all the mango sauce ingredients, except the chili powder, in a mini food processor and blend until smooth.

3. Heat 2 tablespoons coconut oil in a large, nonstick skillet over high heat. While the oil heats, drain the fish of its marinade and discard the marinade. Place the fish slices in the pan individually and panfry in two batches, if necessary. You should hear a loud sizzle when they are added, after which you can decrease the heat to medium-high. Do not turn or move the fish until you see them turn golden brown on the side, about 5 minutes. Season a small pinch of salt, then carefully and gently turn the fish to fry on the other side. Once it's done, transfer to a large plate.

4. PREPARE THE SCALLION-DILL OIL: If needed, add an additional 2 tablespoons coconut oil to the hot skillet used for the fish. Add the scallions and dill and give a gentle toss until the scallions and dill have wilted, about 15 seconds. Season with a small pinch of sea salt.

5. Pour the scallion-dill oil over the fish and serve with fresh cilantro, lime wedges, chopped nuts, if using, and the mango dipping sauce.

WEEK

BATCH COOK

WEEKEND

EASY

FLAVOR

NIGHT BFF

ING PERFECT

FUN

ADD-ONS

POP

Many people think that eating Paleo is all about meat. In fact, it's totally the OPPOSITE. In my Paleo, clean-eating world, dark leafy greens come first. Every meal comes with a healthy side, if not two, and even my meat-loving husband asks for these Easy Add-On side dishes all the time.

Try my Triple Green Kale Salad (page 150), Thai Brussels Sprouts Stir-Fry (page 153), or Chilled Korean Zucchini Slices (page 154).

They bring new flavor twists to these everyday vegetables and will be sure to wow your taste buds!

SESAME GINGER CHOPPED CHICKEN SALAD

ACTIVE TIME: 20 MINUTES | SERVES 2

CHICKEN (SEE NOTE):

1 pound skinless, boneless chicken breasts or thighs or store-bought rotisserie chicken

¼ teaspoon coarse sea salt

¼ teaspoon onion powder

¼ teaspoon garlic powder

⅛ teaspoon dried thyme

⅛ teaspoon red chili powder (optional)

SALAD:

3 to 4 Persian cucumbers, quartered lengthwise and chopped

1 large or 2 medium carrots, sliced into thin matchsticks

2 scallions (or more if you'd like), chopped

½ cup lightly toasted nuts, such as slivered almonds

Mixed leafy greens of your choice

¼ cup I Heart Umami Sesame Ginger Sauce (page 189)

Lightly toasted almonds for garnish

This super simple yet flavorful salad is the perfect dish when you are in a hurry. It makes a wonderful light meal or can be paired with any of the soups in this book. The dressing can be made ahead of time and stored in the refrigerator for up to 2 weeks.

1. COOK THE CHICKEN: Season the raw chicken with the salt, herbs, and spices. Grill until the chicken is completely cooked through and then slice. If using store-bought rotisserie chicken, cut into bite-sized pieces.

2. ASSEMBLE THE SALAD: Layer the chicken over a bed of the tossed salad ingredients, drizzle with the sauce, and garnish with the almonds.

Note

You can substitute any of your favorite chicken seasonings.

TRIPLE GREEN KALE SALAD

ACTIVE TIME: 15 MINUTES | SERVES 4

KALE:

8 to 10 ounces lacinato kale (Tuscan kale)

2 teaspoons toasted sesame oil

2 teaspoons extra virgin olive oil or flaxseed oil

2 small garlic cloves, grated or crushed

1 teaspoon grated fresh ginger

Pinch of coarse sea salt

SALAD:

Large handful of snow peas, chopped

2 teaspoons coconut aminos

2 teaspoons aged balsamic vinegar

1 ripe avocado, peeled, pitted, and sliced

Small handful of scallions, chopped

1 teaspoon orange zest

Hemp seeds (as much as you'd like)

A simple and wonderful way to bring new flavor to everyday kale salad. I add Asian aromatics and gently rub the seasonings and oil into the kale leaves. This dish is not only gorgeous, but also fiber rich. It goes well with any savory main dish.

1. PREPARE THE KALE: Rinse the kale thoroughly. Pat dry. Lay a kale leaf on a cutting board and run a paring knife along each side of the center stem. Repeat until all the stems have been removed. Stack four or five layers of kale leaves, roll them up, and slice into thin strips.

2. In a large bowl, combine the chopped kale leaves with the remaining kale ingredients. Gently massage the kale, rubbing the oil into the leaves for a few seconds.

3. ASSEMBLE THE SALAD: Add the salad ingredients to the kale. Give a quick toss and serve at room temperature or slightly chilled.

THAI BRUSSELS SPROUTS STIR-FRY

ACTIVE TIME: 25 MINUTES | SERVES 4

2 tablespoons coconut aminos

1 teaspoon fish sauce (Red Boat brand preferred; see note)

Small pinch of ground white pepper (optional)

1 teaspoon sea salt

4 cups Brussels sprouts, bottoms trimmed, halved (or quartered if large)

1 tablespoon coconut oil or cooking fat of your choice

2 to 3 large garlic cloves, minced

1 small Thai red chile or Fresno or serrano chile, seeded and finely chopped

Note

For a more Chinese flavor, skip the fish sauce and add a little extra coarse salt.

I love using ingredients that are accessible and easy to find. This Thai-inspired Brussels sprouts stir-fry will bring new exciting flavor to your dinner table. It's a wonderful add-on side dish that tastes great at room temperature or slightly chilled.

1. Bring a large pot of water to a boil.

2. Mix together the coconut aminos, fish sauce, and white pepper, if using, in a small bowl and set aside.

3. Add the sea salt to the boiling water. Add the Brussels sprouts and quickly blanch them for about 1 minute. Remove from the pot. Drain and shock in ice cold water. Set aside to drain.

4. Heat 1 tablespoon of the coconut oil in a large sauté pan over high heat, then lower the heat to medium. Add the garlic and chile and sauté until fragrant, 8 to 10 seconds.

5. Add the Brussels sprouts and sauté for about 30 seconds. Add the coconut aminos mixture and sauté until the sprouts are tender but still crunchy, about 1 minute.

6. Serve at room temperature or slightly chilled.

CHILLED KOREAN ZUCCHINI SLICES

TOTAL TIME: 35 MINUTES | SERVES 5 TO 6

3 medium zucchini, sliced into disks a little less than ¼ inch thick

1½ teaspoons fine sea salt

1½ tablespoons avocado oil

2 teaspoons finely minced garlic

1 tablespoon chopped green scallion (or more if you prefer)

1 teaspoon toasted sesame oil

2 teaspoons sesame seeds (or more if you prefer)

I absolutely adore this side dish whenever my husband, Nate, and I eat out in local Korean restaurants. This dish is inspired by our favorite Korean restaurant in Flushing, Queens. It's perfect for advance preparation and tastes even better the day after. I highly recommend that you give this wonderful side dish a try!

1. Sprinkle the salt over the sliced zucchini and use your hands to gently rub it evenly into each slice. Set aside for about 30 minutes. The salt will pull the water out of the zucchini. After 30 minutes, gently squeeze out the water.

2. Heat the avocado oil in a large skillet over medium heat, then lower the heat to medium-low, add the zucchini, and stir-fry for 3 to 4 minutes, or until the zucchini becomes slightly softer.

3. Add the garlic, green scallion, sesame oil, and sesame seeds. Stir-fry for another 2 minutes and turn off the heat. Taste to see whether more salt is needed.

4. This is best served chilled or at room temperature.

ZUCCHINI CARROT FRITTERS

ACTIVE TIME: 30 MINUTES | SERVES 2

FRITTERS:

2 cups shredded or grated zucchini

2 cups shredded or grated carrot

Fine sea salt

3 large eggs

⅔ cup finely ground almond flour

½ cup sliced scallion, plus more for serving

Freshly ground black pepper

Avocado or coconut oil

PALEO SOUR CREAM:

One 14-ounce can full-fat coconut milk (refrigerated overnight to thicken)

1½ tablespoons fresh lemon juice

1½ teaspoons cider vinegar

Fine sea salt

These lovely veggie fritters remind me of Chinese scallion pancakes. I pair them with a dairy-free Paleo sour cream for a lovely, refreshing taste. These fritters are also great as savory snacks, side dish, or add-ons to your lunch boxes!

1. PREPARE THE FRITTERS: Place the shredded zucchini and carrot in a large bowl. Sprinkle lightly with salt. Set aside for 10 minutes.

2. Use a cheesecloth or your hands to squeeze out as much liquid as you can. Add the eggs, almond flour, scallion, additional salt, and pepper. Stir the mixture until combined.

3. Heat 1½ tablespoons avocado oil in a large skillet over medium-high heat.

4. Scoop about 3 tablespoons of the vegetable mixture per fritter into the pan. Gently press the fritter scoops into round and slightly flattened disks. Cook until golden brown, flipping to cook the other side. Transfer the fritters to a large plate lined with paper towels.

5. While the fritters are frying, make the Paleo sour cream: Separate the thick coconut cream from the thin liquid, discarding the liquid and placing the cream in a bowl. Add the lemon juice, cider vinegar, and sea salt to taste. Whisk until smooth.

6. Serve the pancakes with the Paleo sour cream and sprinkle with scallions.

CHILLED JAPANESE SESAME SPINACH

ACTIVE TIME: 5 TO 10 MINUTES | SERVES 3

Salt

1 large bunch fresh spinach

Toasted sesame seeds (optional)

SESAME SAUCE:

1½ tablespoons tahini

2 tablespoons coconut aminos

1 garlic clove, grated

1 teaspoon rice vinegar

1 teaspoon toasted sesame oil

Whenever Nate and I visit Japanese restaurants, we always order a small plate of chilled sesame spinach as an appetizer. It's light, low-carb, and refreshing. You can easily replicate it at home and it will become one of your family's favorites!

1. Bring a pot of water to a boil. Season the water with a pinch of salt.

2. IN THE MEANTIME, PREPARE THE SESAME SAUCE: Mix together the sauce ingredients with 1½ tablespoons water (add more for a thinner sauce) in a small bowl and set aside.

3. Rinse the spinach. Roughly cut the whole bunch of spinach into three to four large sections.

4. Quickly blanch the spinach in the boiling water for 10 to 15 seconds. Drain and rinse under cold water to stop the cooking and preserve the vibrant color.

5. Gently squeeze the spinach with your hands to remove all of the excess water. Place the spinach in a serving bowl. Drizzle with the sesame sauce and give the spinach a quick toss. Sprinkle with toasted sesame seeds before serving, if desired.

CARROT NOODLES WITH CREAMY TAHINI DRESSING

ACTIVE TIME: 5 MINUTES | SERVES 2

2 large carrots

2 tablespoons tahini

1½ tablespoons coconut aminos

Fresh lemon juice

This is one of my favorite ways to enjoy healthy, low-carb carrot noodles. The dressing is creamy and lemony. The dressed noodles are a wonderful addition to any savory main dish or salad bowl!

1. Use a vegetable peeler to make wide, flat carrot noodles. Place in a medium bowl.

2. Combine the remaining ingredients in a separate bowl with 1½ tablespoons water, stir well, and drizzle over the noodles, Let the noodles soak up the sauce. Refrigerate for 10 to 15 minutes.

3. Enjoy cold.

SIMPLE CAULI FRIED RICE

ACTIVE TIME: 10 TO 15 MINUTES | SERVES 2 TO 3

½ cauliflower, separated into florets (see note)

1 carrot, roughly chopped

1 tablespoon ghee or avocado oil

2 to 3 scallions, chopped and separated into white and green parts

2 small garlic cloves, finely chopped

Coarse salt

¼ teaspoon grated fresh ginger

2 teaspoons coconut aminos

1 teaspoon toasted sesame oil

Toasted white sesame seeds (optional)

Paleo Asian-inspired cauliflower fried rice couldn't get any simpler. Just add some simple seasonings and grated ginger for a quick Asian-flair fried "rice"!

1. Use a food processor to lightly pulse the cauliflower florets and carrot a few times until they are about the size of a large grain of rice.

2. Heat the ghee in a skillet over medium-high heat, then lower the heat to medium and add the white scallion parts and garlic. Season with a small pinch of salt. Sauté until fragrant, 8 to 10 seconds. Add the cauliflower and carrot rice, ginger, coconut aminos, and sesame oil. Season with a small pinch of salt.

3. Stir-fry quickly to cook the cauliflower rice to a slightly softer (but not mushy) texture. Turn off the heat and stir in the green scallion parts. Sprinkle with toasted sesame seeds before serving, if desired.

Note

To save time, you can use 2 cups of store-bought cauliflower rice.

QUICK GARLIC-GINGER KALE SAUTÉ

ACTIVE TIME: 15 MINUTES | SERVES 3 TO 4

1½ to 2 tablespoons avocado oil

2 garlic cloves, finely chopped

Coarse salt

1 large bunch curly kale (10 to 12 ounces), stemmed, leaves coarsely chopped

1 to 2 teaspoons grated fresh or frozen ginger (see note)

A simple way to bring new flavor to kale and everyday sautéed vegetables.

1. Heat a large skillet over medium-high heat, then lower the heat to medium and add the avocado oil and garlic. Season with a small pinch of salt and sauté until fragrant, 6 to 8 seconds.

2. Add the chopped kale and keep sautéing until the leaves turn a darker green but are not withered. Season with another small pinch of salt. Turn off the heat and, while the skillet is still hot, grate about 1 to 2 teaspoons of ginger over the kale (use more if you like). Serve at room temperature or slightly chilled.

Note

Sometimes it's difficult to figure out how to store small pieces of leftover ginger. In this case, I freeze them and use them to grate over different dishes. It gives a light gingery flavor pop to sautéed veggies.

SHIITAKE MUSHROOM AND BABY BOK CHOY STIR-FRY

ACTIVE TIME: 10 MINUTES | SERVES 4

1½ tablespoons avocado oil, plus more if needed

3 garlic cloves, finely minced

1 teaspoon grated fresh ginger

1 Fresno or serrano chile, seeded and finely chopped (optional)

Salt

5 to 6 fresh shiitake mushrooms, stems removed and caps sliced (if using rehydrated shiitakes, use 4 caps)

¾ pound baby bok choy, halved lengthwise (or quartered, if large) and rinsed

Sesame seeds

1 teaspoon toasted sesame oil

This is one of my top go-to vegetable dishes when I'm in a hurry. You can use fresh or rehydrated shiitake mushrooms for an extra umami flavor boost. Don't like mushrooms? Simply omit them for a quick, garlicky baby bok choy stir-fry. This side dish tastes great at room temperature or chilled.

1. Heat the avocado oil in a wok over high heat, then lower the heat to medium, add the garlic, ginger, and red chile, and quickly season with a small pinch of salt. Stir-fry for 8 to 10 seconds, or until fragrant (be careful not to burn the ingredients).

2. Add the mushrooms. Continue stirring and flipping for another minute, or until the mushrooms are softer. Add a bit more oil, if necessary.

3. Add the baby bok choy and cook until it turns light green yet is still crunchy, 1 to 2 minutes. Season with another pinch of salt. Sprinkle with sesame seeds and drizzle with the toasted sesame oil before serving.

SIMPLY ROASTED KALE CHIPS

ACTIVE TIME: 10 MINUTES | BAKE TIME: 10 TO 15 MINUTES | SERVES 2

1 large bunch curly green and/or purple kale (about 1 pound)

2 tablespoons hazelnut or avocado oil

Seasonings of choice (mine are garlic powder, onion powder, smoked paprika, and pink salt or sea salt)

Note

For variety, try sprinkling with nutritional yeast before and after baking to add more flavor!

Kale chips are easy, quick, and perfect healthy snacks. Enjoy them between meals or add to meal bowls for extra-crispy deliciousness.

1. Preheat the oven to 300°F. Line two large baking sheets with parchment paper.

2. Cut away any large stems from the kale. Rinse and thoroughly dry the leaves. Use a salad spinner, if you have one, to help dry the leaves even further.

3. Spread the kale in a single layer on the prepared baking sheets. Lightly brush each leaf both front and back with hazelnut oil. Sprinkle with your seasonings of choice, using your hands to distribute and gently rub the seasonings into both the front and back. Try to make the leaves as flat as possible (not folded over) and leave some space between them.

4. Bake for 10 to 15 minutes, or until the kale is crispy and slightly golden brown. Watch closely as it can burn easily.

5. Remove from the oven and let cool slightly; the leaves will crisp up even more once out of the oven. Use kitchen scissors to cut along any stems. Enjoy immediately. Best when fresh.

SMOKY CURLY SWEET POTATO NOODLE FRIES

ACTIVE TIME: 10 MINUTES | BAKE TIME: 20 TO 25 MINUTES | SERVES 4

2 medium jewel yams or white sweet potatoes (select long, cylindrical potatoes)

3 tablespoons avocado oil

½ teaspoon smoked paprika

½ teaspoon sumac (optional)

¼ teaspoon garlic powder

¼ teaspoon onion powder

Coarse salt

Small handful of chopped fresh parsley

A simple way to enjoy homemade curly noodle fries. Feel free to substitute any other dried seasonings that you like. Experiment with different yams or sweet potatoes for more variety!

1. Preheat the oven to 400°F. Line a large baking sheet with parchment paper.

2. Scrub the yams clean, then spiralize them. (I find it easier to cut them in half widthwise first before spiralizing). Spread out the noodles on the prepared baking sheet, trying not to overlap them too much.

3. Drizzle the spiralized noodles with the avocado oil and all the seasonings, except the parsley. Gently toss to distribute the oil and seasonings evenly.

4. Bake for 20 to 25 minutes, until they turn a light golden brown. Remove from the oven and let cool for 10 to 15 minutes so the texture will firm up more. Sprinkle with the chopped parsley and serve hot.

EASY ROASTED CINNAMON BUTTERNUT SQUASH

ACTIVE TIME: 10 MINUTES | BAKE TIME: 25 MINUTES | SERVES 4

1¼ pounds butternut squash, peeled, seeded, and cut in 1-inch chunks

Olive oil

Coarse sea salt

Vietnamese or Korintje (Indonesian) ground cinnamon

This simple and naturally sweet recipe is absolutely delicious. It's a wonderful add-on dish and provides good carbs when you just need a little pick-me-up. The same recipe and seasonings will work for any other type of squash or sweet potatoes and yams to help you easily create variety.

1. Preheat the oven to 400°F. Line a large baking sheet with parchment paper. Distribute squash cubes evenly over the prepared pan. Drizzle with a good amount of olive oil and season with coarse sea salt to taste. Lightly sprinkle with cinnamon. Use your hands to gently toss the squash and coat the cubes well with the oil and seasonings.

2. Arrange the squash in a single layer and roast for about 25 minutes, or until tender, turning once with a metal spatula midway through roasting.

3. Serve at room temperature or chilled. Store leftovers in a glass container in the refrigerator. Use within 3 days.

LOW-CARB SCALLION PANCAKES

ACTIVE TIME: 25 MINUTES | SERVES 4 (2 SLICES PER PERSON)

½ cauliflower head, separated into florets

2 large eggs

2 tablespoons ground flaxseed meal

¼ teaspoon coarse salt

2 teaspoons coconut aminos

Chopped scallions (at least 3 to 4 bulbs but use as much as you'd like)

Pinch of onion powder

Pinch of ground white pepper (optional)

1 tablespoon avocado oil

⅓ cup I Heart Umami Scallion Pancake Sauce (page 189)

EASY ADD-ONS

Because I love Chinese scallion pancakes so much, I made a low-carb version using cauliflower. Enjoy with my Scallion Pancake Sauce (page 189). They taste just like the real scallion pancakes but won't weigh you down.

1. Place the cauliflower florets in a 4-cup food processor and finely chop to couscous size (see notes). You should have 2 cups of cauliflower rice. Microwave on HIGH for 90 seconds to slightly soften the cauliflower couscous. Set aside to cool, then squeeze out as much liquid as you can with a cheesecloth or clean kitchen towel.

2. Combine the cauliflower in a large bowl with all the remaining ingredients, except the avocado oil and dipping sauce. Mix well and set the mixture aside for 5 to 10 minutes.

3. Meanwhile, heat a 9-inch cast-iron or nonstick skillet (see notes) over low heat, then add the avocado oil and swirl the oil around to grease the skillet evenly. Pour in the pancake batter and quickly and gently spread the mixture evenly around the skillet. Panfry over low heat for about 5 minutes, or until the edge is light golden brown. Make sure it cooks on all sides without burning.

4. Because the pancake is gluten-free, it's a little more fragile than a conventional pancake, so it's helpful if you flip it as follows: when you're ready to flip, hold a flat plate upside down against the top of the pan and invert so the pancake falls out, cooked side up, onto the plate. Put the pan back on the burner and simply let the pancake slide laterally back into the pan. Because the raw side is against the plate, the pancake might leave residue as it slides down. This is normal!

Notes

I find that a 4-cup food processor is best for making 2 cups of cauliflower rice, but a larger one will work as well.

Using a smaller (9-inch) skillet makes it easier to flip the pancake.

continued

5. Cook the flip side for about 3 minutes, or until golden brown, gently shaking the skillet while cooking to keep the flip side from sticking. Slide the pancake out and let cool on a wire rack so that the bottom won't get soggy. Slice into eight wedges and serve at room temperature with the pancake sauce.

FREEZER-FRIENDLY MUFFIN TIN MASHED SWEET POTATO

ACTIVE TIME: 5 MINUTES | COOK TIME: 50 MINUTES (OVEN) OR 20 MINUTES (PRESSURE COOKER) | SERVES 6 PEOPLE

4 to 5 medium sweet potatoes and/or yams (pick those of similar size and shape for even cooking)

One to two 14-ounce cans full-fat coconut milk

Coarse salt

Up to 6 ounces baby spinach (optional)

1 to 2 tablespoons ghee, melted (optional)

From freezer to table in minutes! This easy, make-ahead recipe is perfect for batch cooking. It can be made in either an oven or an electric pressure cooker. No more watery, soggy sweet potato mash!

OVEN METHOD:

1. Preheat the oven to 400°F. Scrub the sweet potatoes clean and use a fork to pierce them a few times all over.

2. Bake for 50 minutes, or until soft when pierced with a fork. Remove from the oven and set aside to cool, then peel the skin away.

3. Transfer the sweet potatoes to a food processor or blender and add ½ can of the coconut milk and a little coarse salt. Blend until your desired creamy consistency is reached. Add more coconut milk, 2 tablespoons at a time, for a less dense consistency. (You can also blend in the baby spinach and ghee with white sweet potatoes to make the mixture green!)

4. Scoop the mashed potatoes into silicone muffin tin(s) and store flat in the freezer until completely solid (overnight works best). Pop the frozen sweet potatoes out of muffin tin(s) and store them in large resealable plastic bags for easy storage. Store in the freezer until you are ready to serve.

5. TO SERVE: Defrost overnight in the refrigerator or reheat in a microwave on HIGH for 2 to 3 minutes total (stir every minute).

continued

ELECTRIC PRESSURE COOKER METHOD:

1. Scrub the sweet potatoes clean. Place a steamer rack inside an electric pressure cooker and place the sweet potatoes in the steamer. Try not to overfill the pot—leave a little gap between each potato to allow the steam to circulate through during cooking. If the potatoes are too large to fit into the pot, you can slice them in half.

2. Add 1 cup of room-temperature water. Close the lid. Seal the valve. Press MANUAL and set the timer to 20 minutes. When finished cooking, allow the pot to naturally release pressure for 5 minutes, then manually release. Once the potatoes are cool to the touch, peel the skin away.

3. Proceed from step 3 on the previous page.

WEEK

BATCH COOK

WEEKEND

EASY

FLAVOR

NIGHT BFF

ING PERFECT

FUN

ADD-ONS

POP

Creating Paleo Asian-inspired sauces and seasonings is not a difficult task, but to have them taste as close as possible to the original flavor, yet distinct from one another, is not easy to do. I don't have a set formula for my creations but rather follow my taste buds to create these Flavor Pop condiments/sauces/seasonings that make food taste so fragrant.

What you will find when you follow these recipes is a much

cleaner tasting meal without added sugar. These Flavor Pop sauces and dressings will become your favorites. You can easily double the recipe quantities.

I HEART UMAMI CURRY FLAVOR ENHANCER

MAKES ABOUT 1 CUP

2 large garlic cloves

2 shallots

1 thumb-sized piece fresh ginger

1 cup fresh cilantro or parsley

2 red Fresno or serrano chiles, seeded

Zest and juice of ½ lime

2 teaspoons ground turmeric

1 teaspoon sea salt

½ teaspoon fish sauce (Red Boat brand preferred), or 1 small piece anchovy

¼ cup extra virgin olive oil

This mixture will enhance any store-bought curry paste (red, green, or yellow). The curry flavor enhancer is meant to be a bit salty. If your store-bought curry paste is very salty, start by adding a smaller quantity of the enhancer first before adding more. When you mix a few tablespoons of my curry flavor booster into a curry pot, it will make your curry taste amazingly delicious!

Place all the ingredients in a food processor and process until fine. This sauce can be made ahead and stored in ice cube trays in the freezer for up to 4 weeks.

I HEART UMAMI SWEET-AND-SOUR SAUCE

MAKES ABOUT ½ CUP

¼ cup dried apricots, figs, or pitted prunes

⅓ cup canned pineapple juice (do not use heavy syrup)

2 tablespoons coconut aminos

1½ tablespoons rice vinegar, or 2 teaspoons cider vinegar

1½ teaspoons no-salt-added tomato paste

Pinch of sea salt

3 to 4 tablespoons chicken stock or water

This Paleo and Whole30-friendly sweet-and-sour sauce is made with dried apricots and pineapple juice to add natural sweetness. It is great for sweet-and-sour chicken or pork, or even a quick shrimp stir-fry.

1. Place the apricots in a mini food chopper or 4-cup herb chopper and pulse a few times until they are diced into small pieces. You can also use a knife to chop the dried fruit into small pieces.

2. Place the remaining ingredients, except the stock, in a medium saucepan and cook over low heat, stirring occasionally, until the fruit softens, about 10 minutes. Add the stock to the sauce and puree, using an immersion blender, until very smooth and no fruit chunks remain. Store in an airtight glass container in the refrigerator for up to 1 week.

♥ I HEART UMAMI SESAME CHICKEN SAUCE

MAKES ABOUT ⅓ CUP

6 Medjool dates, pitted

1 small garlic clove

1 teaspoon grated fresh ginger

3 tablespoons coconut aminos

2 teaspoons rice vinegar

1 tablespoon tomato paste

1 teaspoon hot chili sauce (optional)

1 teaspoon toasted sesame oil

1 tablespoon water

This is my healthy take on the traditional sesame chicken sauce. It is naturally sweetened with dates. You can use the same sesame sauce not only for chicken stir-fries but also for beef, pork, or shrimp.

Place the dates, garlic, and ginger in a small food processor and pulse a few times until finely chopped. Add the rest of the sauce ingredients. Blend a few more times until the sauce is smooth and no fruit chunks remain. Store in an airtight glass container in the refrigerator for up to 2 weeks.

♥ I HEART UMAMI NO-CHOPPING BEEF MARINADE

MAKES MARINADE FOR 1 POUND OF BEEF

2 tablespoons coconut aminos

1½ teaspoons fish sauce (Red Boat brand preferred)

2 to 3 teaspoons toasted sesame oil

¼ teaspoon freshly ground black pepper (optional)

This is my go-to beef marinade and I call it my beef marinade holy trinity. Since Asian dishes emphasize quick stir-fry, this sauce works perfectly for skirt steak and sirloin cuts. If you are rushed for time, these four ingredients are all you need.

Combine all the ingredients in a small bowl and pour over your beef. Allow to marinate for at least 20 minutes (or overnight) for extra flavor. Store in an airtight glass container in the refrigerator for up to 2 weeks.

I HEART ♥ UMAMI TERIYAKI SAUCE

MAKES ABOUT ⅓ CUP

¼ cup apple juice

3½ tablespoons coconut aminos

2 tablespoons cider vinegar

1 teaspoon grated fresh ginger

1 teaspoon grated fresh garlic

1 to 1½ teaspoons arrowroot flour

A simple way to make teriyaki sauce with no added sugar or starch. Slightly warming the sauce enhances the savory flavor and brings out natural sweetness from the coconut aminos and cider vinegar.

Combine all the ingredients in a small saucepan, mixing until there are no lumps. Gently warm over medium-low heat, stirring frequently with a wooden spoon until slightly thickened, 1 to 2 minutes. Store in an airtight glass container in the refrigerator for up to 2 weeks.

I HEART ♥ UMAMI SESAME BEEF SAUCE

MAKES ABOUT ⅓ CUP

¼ cup coconut aminos

¼ cup fresh orange juice

2 tablespoons rice vinegar

1 tablespoon toasted sesame oil

2 teaspoons fish sauce (Red Boat brand preferred)

1 teaspoon tomato paste

2 garlic cloves, grated or crushed

1 tablespoon grated fresh ginger

This Paleo and Whole30-friendly sesame beef sauce is naturally sweet, tart, and savory. I use fresh orange juice to add natural sweetness, fish sauce for extra umami savory taste, and tomato paste for a lovely consistency and a hint of acidity. The flavor combination of fish sauce and coconut aminos works great for any beef recipe.

Combine all the ingredients in a medium saucepan. Reduce the sauce over medium-low to low heat, stirring frequently, to about ⅓ cup, 4 to 5 minutes. The sauce should become glossy in texture. Set aside to cool. Store in an airtight glass container in the refrigerator for up to 2 weeks.

I HEART ♥ UMAMI PALEO WORCESTERSHIRE SAUCE

MAKES ABOUT ⅔ CUP

½ cup beef stock

3 tablespoons tomato paste

2 tablespoons coconut aminos

1 tablespoon aged balsamic vinegar

¼ teaspoon onion powder

¼ teaspoon garlic powder

¼ teaspoon mustard powder

⅛ teaspoon sea salt

⅛ teaspoon ground cinnamon

⅛ teaspoon freshly ground black pepper

Traditional store-bought Worcestershire sauce contains barley malt vinegar, spirit vinegar, molasses, sugar, high-fructose corn syrup, and so on. All that sugar and starch is not great for your body. This Paleo and Whole30-friendly version contains no added sugar or starch. The aged balsamic vinegar gives a nice, smooth finish with a hint of natural sweetness.

Combine the ingredients in a small saucepan. Bring to a simmer over medium-low heat, uncovered and stirring frequently, then simmer for a couple of minutes. Remove from the heat and let cool. If rushed, you can also combine the ingredients without heating the mixture; the consistency will be thinner this way. This sauce can be made ahead and stored in an airtight glass container in the refrigerator for up to 2 weeks.

I HEART ♥ UMAMI DIM SUM DUMPLING DIPPING SAUCE

MAKES ABOUT ¼ CUP

2 tablespoons coconut aminos

1 tablespoon rice vinegar

1 teaspoon toasted sesame oil

1 teaspoon grated fresh ginger

An easy and quick way to make soy- and gluten-free dumpling dipping sauce with no added sugar.

Combine all the ingredients in a small bowl and mix well. This sauce can be made ahead and stored in an airtight glass jar in the refrigerator. Use within 1 week for maximum freshness and flavor. Lightly whisk again before using.

I HEART UMAMI SCALLION PANCAKE SAUCE

MAKES ABOUT ⅓ CUP

¼ cup coconut aminos

4 teaspoons rice vinegar

1 teaspoon toasted sesame oil

2 teaspoons hot chili sauce (optional)

1 teaspoon grated fresh ginger (optional)

Sprinkle of chopped scallions

Sprinkle of toasted white sesame seeds

This soy- and gluten-free dipping sauce is savory and tart, with a hint of spiciness. It's a must-have for scallion pancakes.

Combine all the ingredients in a small bowl and mix well. This sauce can be made ahead and stored in an airtight glass jar in the refrigerator. Use within 1 week for maximum freshness and flavor. Lightly stir or whisk the sauce before serving.

I HEART UMAMI SESAME-GINGER SAUCE

MAKES ABOUT ¼ CUP

2½ to 3 tablespoons rice vinegar

2 tablespoons extra virgin olive oil

1 to 2 teaspoons toasted sesame oil

1 tablespoon coconut aminos

¾ tablespoon grated fresh ginger

¼ teaspoon garlic granules

¼ teaspoon onion granules

This is a great sesame ginger sauce that can be used as a salad dressing or dipping sauce. Use it for grilled or poached chicken, fish fillets, steak, or over salads.

Combine all the ingredients in a small bowl and mix well. This sauce can be made ahead and stored in an airtight glass jar in the refrigerator. Use within 1 week for maximum freshness and flavor. Shake before using.

I HEART UMAMI SCALLION-GINGER DIPPING OIL

MAKES ABOUT ⅔ CUP

⅓ cup avocado oil

5 garlic cloves, thinly sliced

1 medium shallot, minced

1 tablespoon thinly sliced fresh ginger (matchsticks)

4 scallions, chopped and separated into white and green parts

1½ teaspoons coarse salt, or to taste

This dipping oil is inspired by my travels in Hong Kong and Malaysia, where it is often served as a condiment for steamed seafood, boiled chicken, or noodle soup. The aromatics are panfried in avocado oil until fragrant. Think of it as a fragrant oil that can be used for any vegetable stir-fry as well.

1. Heat the avocado oil in a small heavy-bottomed saucepan. Test the oil temperature by adding one slice of garlic: if it starts bubbling right away, that means the temperature is correct. If the garlic burns too quickly, that means the temperature is too hot and the heat should be lowered.

2. Add the garlic, shallot, ginger, and white scallion parts to the oil. Cook until softened, stirring frequently to prevent them from burning. Season with salt to taste. You'll want to aim on the slightly saltier side as this is a dipping sauce meant for plain boiled or steamed chicken, seafood (shrimp, white fish fillets), and/or vegetables (carrots, asparagus).

3. Once the mixture has softened and you can smell a nice aroma, turn off the heat. Stir in the green scallion parts and remove from the heat to let cool.

4. Serve the infused oil at room temperature. Store any extra in an airtight glass container in the refrigerator for up to 2 weeks. Allow it to come to room temperature before using.

I HEART UMAMI MALAYSIAN-INSPIRED CHILI DIPPING SAUCE

MAKES ABOUT ½ CUP

1 whole roasted red bell pepper in oil

½ red Fresno or serrano chile, seeded (optional)

2 small garlic cloves

One 1-inch piece fresh ginger

2 tablespoons rice vinegar

2 to 3 tablespoons chicken stock

½ teaspoon salt

1 teaspoon arrowroot or tapioca starch (optional; see note)

I love how simple it is to make this sauce. Its texture is meant to be a bit runny and it makes a great dipping sauce for crispy wings. If you prefer a thicker texture, warm the sauce over the stovetop to reduce the liquid further.

Place all the ingredients in a food processor or blender and process until smooth. Use the sauce right away or store in a glass jar in the refrigerator. Use within 1 week for maximum flavor and freshness.

Note

The dipping sauce is meant to be a bit runny, so if you prefer a thicker sauce, add a teaspoon of arrowroot or tapioca starch to thicken it.

WEEKLY
MEAL PREP

To make it even easier to plan and prepare a variety of fresh, bold, healthy meals in no time, I have put together four weeks of meal-planning menus with consolidated shopping lists. In addition to the shopping lists, this section includes tips on how to make ahead, store, and reheat the meal-planning recipes. To prepare even more healthy meals, any of these recipes can be easily doubled.

WEEK 1

ENTRÉE 1: Beef and Broccoli (page 52)

ENTRÉE 2: Super Flavorful Easy Chicken Curry (page 92) with I Heart Umami Curry Flavor Enhancer (page 184)

SIDE: Quick Garlic-Ginger Kale Sauté (page 165)

PROTEIN:

½ pound skinless, boneless chicken breasts

1 pound beef (sirloin, skirt steak, flank steak, or boneless short ribs)

PRODUCE:

1 large bunch curly kale (about 1½ pounds)

Broccoli (2 full heads of broccoli crowns or prechopped broccoli florets)

6 garlic cloves

2 large shallots

2 large thumb-sized pieces fresh ginger

1 bunch cilantro

2 red chile peppers (I use Fresno or serrano)

1 lime

PANTRY:

Red curry paste (Thai Kitchen brand preferred)

One 14-ounce can full-fat coconut milk

Coarse sea salt and freshly ground black pepper

Ground turmeric

Arrowroot starch or sweet potato powder

Olive or avocado oil, and/or ghee

Baking soda

Curry powder

Fish sauce (Red Boat brand preferred), or 1 small piece anchovy

Coconut aminos

Toasted sesame oil

FOR THE BEEF AND BROCCOLI:

1. Prepare and cook the Beef with Broccoli up to 3 days ahead, following the instructions on page 52. Pack each serving into individual containers.

2. To reheat, microwave on HIGH in 1-minute increments and stir, until hot.

FOR SUPER FLAVORFUL EASY CHICKEN CURRY:

1. Prepare the Easy Chicken Curry up to 3 days ahead, following the instructions on page 92. Pack each serving into a container. Store for up to 3 days in the refrigerator or up to 3 weeks in the freezer.

2. To reheat, microwave on LOW in 1-minute increments, and stir until the curry is warm. Alternatively, reheat on the stovetop over medium or low heat.

FOR QUICK GARLIC-GINGER KALE SAUTÉ:

1. The kale sauté tastes best when it's fresh out of the stir-fry skillet. To jump-start your cooking, wash and pat the kale leaves dry and coarsely chop them. Store the leaves in a large vegetable produce container or large resealable plastic bags. If using bags, squeeze out the air and store in the refrigerator up to 3 days.

2. When you are ready to eat, rinse the kale leaves and follow the instructions on page 165.

WEEK 2

ENTRÉE 1: Sweet-and-Sour Chicken (page 79) with I Heart Umami Sweet-and-Sour Sauce (page 185)

ENTRÉE 2: Japanese Hamburger Steak (page 111) with I Heart Umami Paleo Worcestershire Sauce (page 188)

SIDE: Chilled Korean Zucchini Slices (page 154)

PROTEIN:

⅔ pound ground beef

⅔ pound ground pork

2 large eggs

1¼ pounds skinless, boneless chicken breasts or thighs

PRODUCE:

4 portobello mushroom caps

1 large red bell pepper and/or 1 large green bell pepper (you will need 1 whole pepper for the chicken)

3 medium zucchini

1 cucumber (optional topping for hamburger)

Small red radishes (optional topping for hamburger)

1 large yellow onion

2 scallions

1 thumb-sized piece fresh ginger

PANTRY:

Salt and freshly ground black pepper

Ground nutmeg

Aged balsamic vinegar

Arrowroot starch or sweet potato flour

Coconut aminos

Onion powder

Mustard powder

Garlic powder

Ground cinnamon

White pepper

Ground ginger

Toasted sesame oil

Toasted white sesame seeds

Rice vinegar or cider vinegar

Almond flour

One 14-ounce can full-fat coconut milk

½ cup beef stock

¼ cup chicken stock (optional)

3 tablespoons tomato paste

⅓ cup canned pineapple juice (do not use heavy syrup)

¼ cup dried apricots, figs, or prunes

Avocado oil or ghee

Olive oil

FOR THE SWEET-AND-SOUR CHICKEN:

1. Following the recipe on page 79, thinly slice the chicken breasts or dice the chicken thighs. Mix well with the remaining chicken ingredients. Divide between two large resealable plastic bags. Push out the air, seal the bags, and store flat in the refrigerator overnight or in the freezer for up to 2 weeks.

2. Prepare the Sweet-and-Sour Sauce up to 1 week ahead, following the instructions on page 185, and store in the refrigerator.

3. When you are ready to eat, defrost one or both bags of chicken in the refrigerator the night before with a flat plate underneath.

4. Prepare the vegetables and cook the chicken following the instructions on page 79. You'll have dinner ready in 15 minutes!

FOR THE JAPANESE HAMBURGER STEAK:

1. Prepare the uncooked hamburger patties up to 1 week ahead, following the instructions on page 111. Alternate the uncooked patties and squares of parchment paper. Store the patties flat in resealable plastic freezer bags, label with the date, and freeze.

2. Prepare the Paleo Worcestershire Sauce up to 2 weeks ahead, following the instructions on page 188, and store in the refrigerator.

3. When you are ready to eat, defrost the patties the night before in the refrigerator with a flat plate underneath, then cook the patties and prepare the vegetables following the instructions on page 111.

FOR THE CHILLED KOREAN ZUCCHINI SLICES:

Prepare the zucchini up to 3 days ahead, following the instructions on page 154, and store in the refrigerator.

WEEK 3

ENTRÉE 1: Lion's Head Meatballs (page 98)

ENTRÉE 2: Savory Taiwanese Roasted Chicken Thigh Steaks (page 88)

SIDE: Triple Green Kale Salad (page 150)

PROTEIN:

1½ pounds ground pork (80% lean, 20% fat, or 70% lean, 30% fat)

4 boneless chicken thighs, skin on (about 2 pounds)

2 large eggs

PRODUCE:

¼ Napa or savoy cabbage

2 to 3 baby bok choy (optional)

8 to 10 ounces lacinato kale (Tuscan kale)

1 large handful of snow peas

1 avocado

1 teaspoon orange zest (optional)

5 scallions

1 large shallot

2 large thumb-sized pieces fresh ginger

6 garlic cloves

1 lemon

PANTRY:

Coarse sea salt and freshly ground black pepper

Coconut aminos

Aged balsamic vinegar

Toasted sesame oil

Extra virgin olive or flaxseed oil

Avocado oil

Cooking spray

About 1 cup chicken or vegetable stock

Arrowroot starch

Hemp seeds

FOR THE LION'S HEAD MEATBALLS:

1. Prepare and cook the meatballs and cabbage up to 3 to 4 days ahead, following the instructions on page 98. Once they are cool, pack each serving into a container and store in the refrigerator.

2. When you are ready to eat, reheat them in a large soup pot or Dutch oven on the stovetop over medium heat until the broth is bubbling and the meatballs are warm.

FOR TAIWANESE SAVORY ROASTED CHICKEN THIGH STEAKS:

1. Prepare and roast the chicken thigh steaks following the instructions on page 88. Once they are cool, pack each serving into a container in the refrigerator.

2. When you are ready to eat, either reheat in the broiler on HIGH for 3 to 4 minutes or quickly sear over the stovetop until the chicken is sizzling hot.

FOR TRIPLE GREEN KALE SALAD:

1. The kale salad tastes best when it's freshly made. To prep, pat the kale leaves dry and tear them into bite-sized pieces. Store the leaves in a large vegetable produce container or large resealable plastic bags. If using bags, squeeze out the air and store in the refrigerator up to 3 days.

2. When you are ready to eat, rinse the kale leaves, then follow the instructions on page 150 to finish the seasonings.

WEEK 4

ENTRÉE 1: Crispy Sesame Beef (page 107) with I Heart Umami Sesame Beef Sauce (page 187)

ENTRÉE 2: Chinese Meat Sauce with Eggplant (page 97)

SIDE: Shiitake Mushroom and Baby Bok Choy Stir-Fry (page 166)

PROTEIN

1 pound sirloin steak

½ pound ground pork + ½ pound ground chicken or turkey, or omit the pork and use 1 pound ground chicken or turkey (Mix breast and thigh meat to make it tastier.)

PRODUCE:

2 to 3 medium Italian eggplants, or carrots and celery

¾ pound baby bok choy

5 to 6 fresh shiitake mushroom caps

6 large garlic cloves

2 thumb-sized pieces fresh ginger

1 large shallot

3 scallions

1 fresh red Fresno or serrano chile (optional)

¼ navel orange (for ¼ cup fresh orange juice)

See pages 97 and 107 for optional vegetables

PANTRY:

Coarse sea salt and freshly ground black pepper

Red pepper flakes (optional)

Coconut aminos

Rice vinegar

Aged balsamic vinegar

Fish sauce (Red Boat brand preferred)

Toasted sesame oil

Ghee and avocado oil

Toasted white sesame seeds

Arrowroot starch

Garlic granules

Onion granules

1 tablespoon tomato paste

About ½ cup chicken or vegetable stock

FOR THE CRISPY SESAME BEEF:

1. Prepare the Crispy Sesame Beef up to 4 days ahead, following the instructions on page 107. Once cool, pack each serving into a container in the refrigerator.

2. When you are ready to eat, microwave on HIGH in 1-minute increments and stir until the beef is hot. Or reheat in a skillet over medium-high heat.

FOR CHINESE MEAT SAUCE WITH EGGPLANT:

1. Prepare the Chinese Meat Sauce with Eggplant up to 4 days ahead, following the instructions on page 97. Once cool, pack each serving into a container in the refrigerator.

2. When you are ready to eat, microwave on HIGH in 1-minute increments and stir until the meat sauce is hot.

FOR SHIITAKE MUSHROOM AND BABY BOK CHOY STIR-FRY:

1. Prepare and sauté the Shiitake Mushroom and Baby Bok Choy Stir-Fry up to 2 days ahead, following the instructions on page 166. Once cool, pack into glass containers and store in the refrigerator.

2. Serve at room temperature or chilled.

ACKNOWLEDGMENTS

A huge thank-you to Aurora Bell for putting up with me and my taking forever to write this book—and my grammar! Without you, this book would never have happened. Thank you for organizing my thoughts and ideas, and for teaching me how to write like a real author; you made this book the best it could be. Thanks a million!

I also would like to thank Jess Murphy, Devon Zahn, and everyone at The Countryman Press for helping to create a cookbook that I am beyond excited about. Thank you to Iris Bass for combing through the book line by line and word by word to bring together a seemingly impossible book. Thank you to LeAnna Weller Smith for your impeccable taste and design, and for your help in landing my first cookbook deal!

To my husband, Nate: thank you for putting up with me and not being able to use the kitchen while I'm filming and shooting photographs for the book week after week. But at least you get to eat all the yummy food afterward, right?

To my mom, dad, brother, and grandparents: you are my inspiration for every single meal I've created in this book. I am fortunate to have you by my side. All the childhood memories and every single meal we have shared together made this book possible. My love for you and my home country will never change.

To my two little chihuahuas, Cody and Zoe: thank you for sacrificing your play time because Mommy had to catch the sun or that perfect cloud before it all goes away!

Last, but certainly not least, to my loyal IHeartUmami.com community; my meal planning course members; Instagram, Facebook, YouTube, and Pinterest followers: this book would not have been possible without each and every one of you. I made this cookbook for you and my hope is that it will become a guide that you use daily and that you can share the experience with your family and loved ones for generations to come. Thank you for your super sweet and lovely comments and positive feedback. You guys will always be my favorite people and my internal sunshine!

INDEX

Copyright © 2019 by ChihYu Chiang

All rights reserved
Printed in China

For information about permission to reproduce selections from this book,
write to Permissions, The Countryman Press, 500 Fifth Avenue, New York, NY 10110

For information about special discounts for bulk purchases, please contact
W. W. Norton Special Sales at specialsales@wwnorton.com or 800-233-4830

Manufacturing through Asia Pacific Offset
Book design by LeAnna Weller Smith
Production manager: Devon Zahn

Library of Congress Cataloging-in-Publication Data

Names: Smith, ChihYu, author.
Title: Asian paleo : easy, fresh recipes to make ahead or enjoy right now from I heart umami /
    ChihYu Smith.
Description: New York, NY : Countryman Press, a division of W. W. Norton & Company
    Independent Publishers Since, 1923, [2019] | Includes index. Identifiers: LCCN 2018056044 |
    ISBN 9781682682616 (hardcover)
Subjects: LCSH: Cooking, Asian. | Primitive societies—Food. | Nutrition. | LCGFT: Cookbooks.
Classification: LCC TX724.5.A1 S553 2019 | DDC 641.595—dc23 LC record available at https://
    lccn.loc.gov/2018056044

The Countryman Press
www.countrymanpress.com

A division of W. W. Norton & Company, Inc.
500 Fifth Avenue, New York, NY 10110
www.wwnorton.com

978-1-68268-261-6

10 9 8 7 6 5 4 3 2 1